Hodder Gibson

Scottish Examination Materials

HIGHER ENGLISH

Close Reading

Answers and Marking Schemes

Ann Bridges *and* Colin Eckford

HODDER GIBSON
PART OF HACHETTE LIVRE UK

Orders: please contact Bookpoint Ltd, 130 Milton Park, Abingdon, Oxon OX14 4SB. Telephone: (44) 01235 827720. Fax: (44) 01235 400454. Lines are open 9.00–5.00, Monday to Saturday, with a 24-hour message answering service. Visit our website at www.hoddereducation.co.uk. Hodder Gibson can be contacted direct on: Tel: 0141 848 1609; Fax: 0141 889 6315; email: hoddergibson@hodder.co.uk

© Ann Bridges and Colin Eckford 2007
First published in 2007 by
Hodder Gibson, an imprint of Hodder Education,
part of Hachette Livre UK
2a Christie Street
Paisley PA1 1NB

Impression number   5 4
Year   2010 2009 2008

Cover photo © Image Source / Alamy
Typeset in New Baskerville 11/14pt by Fakenham Photosetting, Fakenham, Norfolk
Printed in Great Britain by Hobbs the Printers, Totton, Hants.

A catalogue record for this title is available from the British Library

ISBN-13: 978-0-340-92816-5

Contents

Marking Guidelines for:

Comparative Evaluation Examples

Introduction

Where appropriate, there are marking guidelines similar to those used for past examinations.

For the supporting, 'lead-in' questions, which are often not of the type asked in the exam, there are detailed answers in a format as close as possible to the one used in traditional Marking Instructions.

It should be remembered that the details and suggestions in these (indeed in nearly all) Guidelines are as much teaching resources as assessment tools, and that they can/should be used in discussion with students after (or before) a task has been undertaken.

Set One

Competitive Sport

Note that there is not a traditional allocation of marks for these questions, although teachers/lecturers setting the task as a formal written exercise could readily allocate as follows, depending on the amount of time students are to be given:

- Question 1 – 1 mark
- Question 2 – 4 or 5 marks
- Question 3(a) – 4 or 5 marks
- Question 3(b) – 1 mark
- Question 3(c) – 4 or 5 marks
- Question 3(d) – 3 or 4 marks
- Question 4(a) – 3 or 4 marks
- Question 4(b) – 5 or 6 marks
- Question 4(c)(i) – 4 or 5 marks
- Question 4(c)(ii) – 2 marks
- Question 5 – 5 or 10 marks

1   **Identify very briefly the key point of similarity in the writers' attitudes to competitive sport.**

They both believe that competitive sport is good for young people, that valuable lessons can be learned from losing, that it is character-building, …

2   **To what extent do you agree with their point of view? Refer to the ideas/examples in the passages and to your own experience.**

Assess the depth of understanding of the writers' opinion, the validity of the student's point(s) of view, and the effectiveness of her/his use of personal experience/knowledge.

3   *(a)* **Read lines 1–23 of Passage One.**

Describe the writer's attitude to the traditional school sports day and show in detail how her choice of language helps to convey this. Refer closely to mood and tone and to how these are created.

The attitude is one of approval, support, that they were enjoyable, uplifting events – although lines 16–18 recognise that this is not universally so.

The mood is of nostalgic recollection, tinged with light mockery of the events and of herself.

Possible language points include:

1	'memories come flooding back'	sense of overwhelming power; nostalgic tone
2	structure of first sentence	colon introduces long list of memories, as if they go on forever

continued ➤

Competitive Sport

3	'rough', 'straining', 'hobbled', 'knotted tightly', 'smell', 'smashing'	clarity of memory in physical detail; range of senses
4	'(in my case, very occasional)'	self-deprecating parenthesis
5	'running full tilt', 'hearts thudding', 'pelted'	sense of speed, exhilaration
6	'trials of strength and skill', 'watch the contest unfold'	connotations of ancient, noble activity
7	'absorbing', 'beautiful', 'thrill'	connotations of excitement, attraction, pleasure
8	'Of course …'	to introduce concession that it is not perfect for everyone
9	'hating', 'being last', 'under pressure', 'too seriously'	connotations of discomfort, suffering to convey feelings of some people
10	example of Jeffrey Archer	to prove the absurdity of some people's attitude
11	'But …'	to indicate return to positive, approving side
12	'joyfully', 'flying', 'simple pleasure'	connotations of enjoyment, gracefulness, … [+ reference to Diana itself suggests youth, beauty, …]

(b) **What function does line 24 perform in the passage as a whole?**

It provides a turning point from (praise of) the traditional sports day to (criticism of) the new 'zone sport day'.

(c) **Read lines 25–55 of Passage One.**

Describe the writer's attitude to the 'zone sport day' and show in detail how her choice of language helps to convey this.

The attitude is critical, scathing, contemptuous, …

Possible language points include:

1	'new concept'	possibly has connotations of something rather over-elaborate or even bogus
2	use of inverted commas	might be to indicate distaste for the term (although could equally be simply because introducing an unfamiliar term)

continued ➤

Competitive Sport

3	'poor, unhappy hodge-podge'	very demeaning tone; element of personification as if a miserable child; connotations of ill-defined, confused, pointless, …; childish sound to suggest something rather silly
4	'does away with'	hints at something destructive, as if getting rid of something valuable
5	'*ad hoc*'	connotations of something rather hasty, temporary, hence unsatisfactory
6	'shamble'	to create impression of ungainly, purposeless movement
7	'not … bothered', 'not … trying', 'completely unaware (of what is happening)'	cumulative picture of children as totally uninvolved, unstimulated, …
8	'supposed (to have the advantage)'	grudging concession, but could be deliberately ironic, since 'supposed' often implies a false claim
9	'tedious … dreary plod … depressing … pointless … boring'	accumulation of critical words stresses how completely awful she thinks it is; 'plod' especially – slow and laboured as opposed to swift, graceful, …
10	'I would rather watch paint drying.'	the ultimate insult; short, forceful sentence heightens impact
11	'One wonders …' + school metaphor	rather whimsical, cynical view of education
12	'shuffle'	connotations of slow, limited, bored, uninvolved activity
13	last sentence	very negative; tone by now almost despairing

(d) **Read lines 56–64 of Passage One.**

Describe the writer's tone in the concluding paragraph and explain in detail how her choice of language helps to convey this tone.

Tone is passionate, almost dogmatic, forceful, …

Possible language points include:

1	'Surely'	direct plea to reader
2	'resurrect'	connotations of restoring something valuable, worthwhile, …

continued ➤

> Competitive Sport

3	short sentences (x3)	dogmatic tone, no argument allowed
4	'for heaven's sake'	as if appealing for common sense
5	'never be out of date'	concludes by emphasising the value of competitive sport as something that will always be of value

4 **(a) Read lines 1–8 of Passage Two.**

How effective do you find this paragraph as an introduction to the article as a whole? Refer to the style and ideas of the paragraph and to the ideas of the passage as a whole.

Possible points:

1. introduces idea that sporting defeat can have serious psychological consequences – this is the idea she goes on to accept, but argue that it is important and valuable

2. uses second person to involve reader; and pretends to instruct reader what to do ('repeat after me')

3. uses an example likely to be familiar to many people in Scotland

4. opens the passage in a fairly light-hearted way – the crassness of McLeod's comments, especially in light of what followed; the idea of a 'benchmark for Scottish ineptitude'; making fun of ourselves as Scots

(b) Read lines 9–30 of Passage Two.

Referring to at least one example from each paragraph, show how the writer's language conveys her attitude to the people behind the changes she is describing.

The attitude is one of contempt, disapproval, …

Possible language points include:

Lines 9–13

1	use of inverted commas round 'football development officers'	slightly sarcastic as if mocking the grandiose nature of the job description
2	'insist'	connotations of being bossy, dogmatic, …

Lines 14–19

3	'banned'	suggests rather dictatorial action
4	'(henceforth to be known as "the runners-up")'	parenthetical aside mocking the euphemistic nature of the new terminology; also, the rather grandiloquent 'henceforth' suggests the pomposity of those behind the term

continued ➢

> ## Competitive Sport

Lines 20–25

5	'rewriting … the rulebook'	connotations of something underhand, unfair, devious, …
6	'officials'	dehumanises them, makes them sound unpleasantly bureaucratic, …
7	'decreed'	makes them sound dictatorial, pompous, …

Lines 26–30

8	'well-meaning'	often/usually implies '… but misguided'
9	'may believe'	with overtones of '… but they're wrong'
10	'… , but' [after list of possible benefits]	underlines her belief they're wrong
11	'sinister'	connotations of something unsavoury, hidden, dangerous, damaging, …

(c) **Read lines 31–50 of Passage Two.**

> *(i)* **Describe in detail how the writer creates a predominantly impassioned and forceful tone in her concluding paragraphs.**

Possible points:

1 the careful structure of lines 31–34: series/list of assertions beginning with 'that …' builds to a mini-climax in 'at all costs'; followed by clearly introduced summary: 'In short, …'; repetition of the 'learn that …' formula; concluding with balanced 'not merely acceptable, it is desirable'; many rhetorical devices to sway reader

2 in lines 35–45 especially, nearly all sentences are purely assertive; little or no evidence or elaboration is offered, implying that her point of view is unquestionable

3 the challenging, aggressive tone of 'You name it'

4 refers to new ideas as 'cruel' – a very emotive word to use in the context of children

5 lines 41–45: deliberately repetitive structure: 'Sport teaches … It allows… It provides… and it teaches…' – again rhetorical appeal to reader's emotions

6 series of 'positive', uplifting words such as 'work together', 'achieve', 'common goal', 'acceptable outlet', 'harness' – to stress the value of competitive sport

7 in final paragraph, emotional reference to 'a weeping child'

continued ➤

Competitive Sport

8   concludes with direct question to reader, but not a question expressing any uncertainty, rather one which demands to be answered: 'You can't', i.e. the writer believes her case is proven beyond doubt. Also the question is structured to sound more convincing by carefully balancing the phrases: 'misery of losing' and 'exhilaration of winning'

(ii) **Identify one point in these paragraphs where the writer's tone is very lighthearted and comment on the effectiveness of this sudden change.**

'breaking wind'

This could be argued as effective because it's rather amusing and this might make a reader more sympathetic to the point the writer is making, or because the abrupt change of tone keeps the reader alert.

On the other hand it could be argued as ineffective because it is jarringly out of place in what appears to be a passionate peroration, or because it is rather crude.

5   **Use your answers to the preceding questions (and any other points you think are relevant) to write a structured response to the following exam-type question:**

Which writer do you think makes the more persuasive case in favour of competitive sport for young people? Justify your choice by referring to the style of writing in each passage.

[Marking Instructions in the style of those for formal tests are given below, but if students have been given a good allocation of time (and this is desirable), it might be sensible to 'double' the marks.]

Note that candidates are instructed to focus on style. Reference to the ideas of the passages is, of course, unavoidable and will in many cases strengthen the candidate's response.

The mark for this question should reflect the overall quality of the response and may not be directly related to the length of the response or to the number of points/references made. A succinct, sophisticated response should be worth more than a series of fairly trivial points and obvious references. 'Ticking and adding up' is not appropriate (or fair) here.

For full marks there must be reference to both passages (although not necessarily a balanced treatment) and convincing evaluative comment. Where reference is made to one passage only, the maximum mark is 3 (6).

The following guidelines should be used:

5 marks (or 9/10 marks)	clear and intelligent understanding of style in both passages; effective references; evaluative comment is convincing
4 marks (or 7/8 marks)	clear understanding of style in both passages; sensible references; evaluative comment is reasonably convincing
3 marks (or 5/6 marks)	understanding of style in both passages; adequate references; discernible evaluative comment

continued ➤

Competitive Sport

2 marks (or 3/4 marks)   some understanding of style; limited reference; at least one appropriate evaluative comment

1 mark (or 1/2 marks)   one or two relevant but unconvincing comments

There should be ample material in the suggestions for Questions 1–4, but all points which students include should be considered on their merits.

In addition to the above, reference could be made to:

- Passage One makes much more use of personal recollection (sports day as a child, zone sports as a parent)

- Passage Two is more distinctly Scottish

- Similar structures: illustrative introduction (the traditional sports day; World Cup 1978), criticism of new trend (zone sports; new rules for school football), peroration in favour of competitive sport.

Set Two

Serving on a Jury

Note that there is not a traditional allocation of marks for these questions, although teachers/lecturers setting the task as a formal written exercise could readily allocate as follows, depending on the amount of time students are to be given:

- Question 1 – 1 or 2 marks
- Question 2 – 2 or 4 marks
- Question 3 – 4 or 6 marks
- Question 4 – 5 or 10 marks

1   Identify very briefly the key difference of opinion about the jury system.

Lewin thinks it is poor, inefficient, unsatisfactory…, while Steel thinks it works well, is commendable …

2   Note other significant points of disagreement (e.g. about the experience of serving on a jury, opinions about fellow jurors, etc.).

Possible answers:

1   Lewin found it disheartening, discouraging ('faith … severely battered'); Steel found it uplifting, inspiring ('exhilarated'). [Point of interest: the headlines given to the published articles were: 'The Depressing Reality of Jury Service' and 'Serving on a Jury Restored my Faith in Humanity'.]

2   Lewin criticises fellow jurors ('deeply ignorant people'); Steel praises them ('inspiring enthusiasm')

3   Lewin claims lack of social spread; Steel mentions an advertising executive, a nurse, (someone who looked like) a headmistress

4   Lewin says 'many … neglected to take notes'; Steel states: 'Everyone had taken notes'

5   Lewin says jurors had 'no analytical ability'; Steel demonstrates (in lines 32–40) quite the opposite, and uses word 'methodically'

6   Lewin sees accused as largely guilty ('no matter how damning the evidence', '"extremely generous" to the accused man', 'obviously guilty criminals'); Steel presents them in sympathetic light ('timid', 'I felt bad for', 'lad')

continued ➤

Serving on a Jury

---

3   **Identify, with examples, key features of each writer's style, paying particular attention to tone.**

Possible points:

Passage one:

Tone:

- frequently sneering, superior-sounding, patronising ('trouble filling out the simplest forms', 'drowning in complexities'; the inverted commas round 'remembering'; 'totally random, haphazard way', 'deeply ignorant people')

- rather irritable tone established early on with 'For a start ...'

- can be reasonably objective, e.g. in lines 54–65 when suggesting improvements

- concludes, however, in very contemptuous tone ('stupid', 'deeply ignorant')

Other features:

- habit of appearing to sound reasonable, make concessions ('you might think', 'I suppose') then countering with a problem ('The trouble was ...' – line 12 and line 18)

- sequence of paragraph openings in lines 30–43 ('I was appalled ...', 'I was also shocked ...', 'But what dismayed me most ...') – sense of sustained attack, building to a climax, use of emotive vocabulary

- the anecdote in lines 22–26 – use of 'accosted' to suggest unpleasant encounter; the rather inconsequential inclusion of gender and age; the use of 'amazement' to stress his superiority; the lack of comment after her response – as if she's too stupid for words; the patronising tone of 'dawn finally on her consciousness'

Important note:

Candidates should be discouraged here, and in all comparison questions, from referring to and analysing small features of language in isolation. For example, the parentheses in lines 3–4 and line 32, the imagery in line 21, the repetition of 'no' in lines 35–36, the minor sentence in line 54, the question in lines 56–57 could all be referred to – but only as a way of supporting a more general point about the writer's style. Comparison questions require students to look at 'the big picture'.

Passage two:

Tone:

- generally light-hearted/humorous (joke about 'bring in games' in opening paragraph, fanciful suggestion in second paragraph, 'the multilingual dope boy', the description of the 'stern woman', the 'nifty slogan', the parody of the non-voter's complaint)

- but capable of being straightforward and fairly serious e.g. in lines 29–40 and lines 49–56 – although rounds off both of these with a one-liner

- warm, positive, uplifting tone towards the end ('beauty of the jury system', 'respond with inspiring enthusiasm', 'skipped', 'exhilarated', 'humanity'; the use of 'lad' – to portray him as unthreatening [contrast closing words of Passage One]; the moving simplicity of the nurse's remark [contrast the out-of-court encounter with a fellow juror related in Passage One])

continued ➤

> *Serving on a Jury*

Other features:

- modest/self-critical – completely wrong about attitude of fellow jurors ('felt certain … would convict) and of the 'stern woman', openly admits others gave 'better examples'

- forcefulness of '– unanimously' (line 57) in driving home point about jury working together

4   Use your answers to the preceding questions (and any other points you think are relevant) to write a structured response to the following exam-type question:

Which writer do you find more effective in making you aware of important issues about jury service? Justify your choice by referring to the ideas and style in each passage.

[Marking Instructions in the style of those for formal tests are given below, but if students have been given a good allocation of time (and this is desirable), it might be sensible to 'double' the marks.]

Note that the question is on 'ideas and style'.

The mark for this question should reflect the overall quality of the response and may not be directly related to the length of the response or to the number of points/references made. A succinct, sophisticated response should be worth more than a series of fairly trivial points and obvious references. 'Ticking and adding up' is not appropriate (or fair) here.

For full marks there must be reference to both elements (i.e. ideas and style) and to both passages (although not necessarily a balanced treatment) and convincing evaluative comment. Where reference is made to one passage only, the maximum mark is 3 (6).

The following guidelines should be followed:

5 marks (or 9/10 marks)	clear and intelligent understanding of both passages; sensible comments on style; evaluative comment is thoughtful and convincing
4 marks (or 7/8 marks)	clear understanding of both passages; sensible comments on style; evaluative comment is reasonably convincing
3 marks (or 5/6 marks)	understanding of both passages; acceptable comment(s) on style; there is some evaluative comment
2 marks (or 3/4 marks)	some understanding of both passages; acceptable comment(s) on style; at least one appropriate comment
1 mark (or 1/2 marks)	one or two relevant but unconvincing comments

Possible points can be found in the suggested answers to question 2 (ideas) and question 3 (style), although all points which candidates propose will have to be judged on their merits.

Set Three

The Importance of Reading

Note that there is not a traditional allocation of marks for these questions, although teachers/lecturers setting the task as a formal written exercise could readily allocate as follows, depending on the amount of time students are to be given:

- Question 1 – 3 marks
- Question 2 – 4 marks
- Question 3 – 5 or 10 marks

1 Identify briefly the key similarity and the key difference in the writers' attitude to reading books.

Both believe that reading is important/gives pleasure to them/others.

Morpurgo believes that reading is important in the development of the individual. Horowitz believes that reading does not in itself make you a good person.

2 To what extent do you think the title of each passage provides an effective introduction to the ideas of the passage?

'Once Upon A Time We Read Our Children Stories' – obvious comment on 'Once Upon A Time' as conventional opening to fairy tales, etc., so a suitable indication that the subject matter will be about stories, literature etc.; use of past tense 'read' indicates this no longer happens – a key point in Morpurgo's complaint; also creates slightly regretful tone at idea of something good now being in the distant past.

'Thou Shalt Read' – imitates 'commandment'-style language to hint at unthinking, dictatorial view that reading must be good for you, which is what Horowitz goes on to question.

3 Which passage do you find more effective in stimulating your thoughts about the importance of reading? You should refer to the ideas and/or style of both passages. (Indicate clearly at the start whether you are referring to ideas or style or to both.)

The wording of this question allows for any one of three different approaches.

Marking Guidelines for **ideas only** can be found with Set Four (pages 18–19).

Marking Guidelines for **style only** can be found with Set One (page 7–8).

Marking Guidelines for **ideas and style** can be found with Set Two (page 11).

The following points could be made, but all points which candidates propose will have to be judged on their merits:

> ## The Importance of Reading

Passage One	Passage Two
Ideas	
• reading can be made enjoyable for children by public events	• intense interest in reading is misplaced
• many, however, are not interested	• Government involvement is suspect
• everyone is to blame for this	• wrong to assume reading makes you a better person
• parents must read to their children	• doubtful quality of much commonly-read material
• teachers have the greatest responsibility to encourage a love of reading	• reading is important to the writer, but it's wrong to force it on everyone in the belief it will be 'improving'
• teachers should be allowed to read stories just for pleasure	
• reading is a vital tool for life	
Style	
• intro from personal experience to draw reader in	• generally rather combative, provocative in tone
• enthusiasm in 'loves ... passion ... sheer joy, fun and wonder ... enriched'	• in opening paragraph mockingly repeats typical questions, then adds his own: 'But who cares'? – surprising, shocking
• series of questions in lines 16–20 to show his concern/perplexity	• cynical question of writer's motives in 'Or film deals and six-figure advances?'
• bluntness of 'Blame someone.'	• 'proclaims' (line 10) – to suggest brash, self-important announcement by Government
• listing in lines 21–29	• critical connotations of 'simplistic' (line 18)
• periodic sentence in lines 21–29	• sentence structure in lines 19–20 imitates simplistic, false logic
• critical nature of 'tools ... drab ... rubbish' (lines 26–28)	• series of questions in lines 22–27 highlights problems of government involvement
• admission that writers are 'complicit'	• sarcastic tone of 'like vitamins...' (line 31)
• imagery of 'mother's milk' (line 36) – essential, basic nutrient ...	• sneering tone in 'their little Gemma' (line 36)
• connotations of 'intimate' (line 36) – complicity etc.	• exaggeration in nine-year-old reading *War and Peace*

The Importance of Reading

- uplifting tone in 'hear the music in the words', 'confidence, fervour and delight', 'delight, inspire' (lines 40–44)

- slogan-like 'literature before literacy' (line 45)

- imagery of 'Unchain … unlock … freedom' (lines 46–47)

- passion/emotion of final paragraph

- provocative tone in lines 39–42: questions, 'Step forward …'; 'literature and crap'

- clarity, simplicity, assertiveness of 'precisely my point' (emphasised by alliteration) and 'Reading is enjoyable.' (line 49)

- sharp contrast in authors referred to in lines 51–52 ('literary'/'popular')

- contrast in personalities referred to in final paragraph (culture/business)

- final sentence – simple statement, admission followed by 'but', delayed by dash, use of 'certainly'…

Set Four

'Public Grief'

Note that there is not a traditional allocation of marks for these questions, although teachers/lecturers setting the task as a formal written exercise could readily allocate as follows, depending on the amount of time students are to be given:

- Question 1 – 1 mark
- Question 2(a) – 5 or 6 marks
- Question 2(b) – 6 or 8 marks
- Question 3(a) – 4 marks
- Question 3(b) – 4 or 6 marks
- Question 4 – 5 or 10 marks

1   Identify very briefly the key point on which the two writers agree.

There is an excess of public grief, it is distasteful/unnecessary/illogical, it is manipulated by the media, …

2   Read Passage One again.

(a) **Explain why Katie Grant 'breathed a sigh of relief' (line 3) in church, and go on to summarise the main points in her argument.**

She was relieved that Mr Bigley's death was given appropriate/tasteful attention by the priest, or that she wasn't being forced to listen to excessive/extravagant praise of him

Main points:

- Mr Bigley has been turned into something he was not
- many people seem unable to deal with death sensibly/rationally
- we are made to feel we have to make our grief public, to be seen to be grieving
- you are likely to be criticised/thought badly of if you do not do this
- the truth about Mr Bigley was hidden/denied
- no one should be forced to grieve

(b) **Show in detail how she makes clear her distaste for what she calls 'coerced grief' (line 31). You should examine especially lines 14–47 and consider such features as word choice, sentence structure and tone.**

Possible answers (from lines 14–47):

1	'prompted, then … obliged'	passive verbs, implying idea comes from others, is forced on us

continued ➤

'Public Grief'

2	'rush about'	connotations of lack of purpose, …
3	'emoting publicly'	implications of falseness, putting on a show, …
4	'signing … buying … lighting'	suggestion of frantic activity; list form to suggest how much has to be (seen to be) done
5	' – all for people we have never met'	dash delays the additional point to emphasise the absurdity of it
6	'manipulated, municipalised … nationalised'	emphasis on control; also sounds very harsh and intrusive
7	'frowned … frowned … frowns'	repetition to convey constant disapproval from critics
8	'self-righteous'	clear suggestion of smug, self-important, …
9	short sentence (line 31)	simple, clear statement of point of view
10	'invidious and false'	highly critical word choice, suggestions of dishonesty, offensiveness, …
11	'pundits'	hints at self-important, self-appointed experts
12	'overblown … rhetoric'	suggests exaggerated, out of proportion and designed (deviously?) to stir emotions
13	short sentence/question (line 41)	dramatic appeal for honesty, criticism of the perceived need to disguise his motives
14	'syrupy veneer'	suggests maudlin superficiality, over-sweet, tacky, …
15	'fake sainthood … attempted canonisation'	exaggeration to emphasise the extent to which Mr Bigley's life/death has been distorted
16	'tainted'	sense of spoiling, contaminating, polluting, …

Further possibilities (from lines 1–13 and 48–56):

17	'cringing' (line 8)	effect of previous mentions of Mr Bigley was deeply embarrassing
18	'manipulated' (line 9)	connotations of being controlled, denied own feelings, …
19	'sugary confection' (line 52)	similar to point 14 above, with suggestion of trying to disguise something, make it more palatable, …

'Public Grief'

---

3   **Read Passage Two again.**

(a) **According to Preston, who is more responsible for the 'Parade of Grief' – the public or the media? Justify your choice by close reference to the passage.**

The question requires students to look closely at Preston's argument. Better answers will argue that Preston seems to hold them responsible in about equal measure, that it started with the public's unpredicted response to the death of Diana, but then the media, unwilling to miss out on a similar phenomenon, ensured that in future high-profile deaths received extensive coverage and that the public are now willing co-conspirators. Nevertheless, it should be possible to come down fairly strongly on either side.

Key references:

*   'We weren't doing it for him; we were doing it for us.'

*   'It seemed utterly spontaneous.'

*   'Joe Public was standing up to be counted'

*   'Nobody was prepared for the moment that followed'

*   'It was another brief encounter with history'

*   'millions of mourners – and thousands of TV cameras.'

*   'the media hearse rolling heedlessly downhill'

*   'Give Joe Public another chance of "being there"'

(b) **Preston's tone is often quite cynical. Give some examples and explain how each example makes the cynicism clear.**

Possible answers:

1	'we were treating ourselves' (line 5)	suggestion of self-indulgence
2	'Joe Public' (line 11)	colloquial, generic name, as if everyone the same
3	'a cocktail of tabloid romance …' (lines 19–20)	suggests confused, heady mixture of mostly superficial elements
4	'But how quickly we learn.' (line 21)	as if we are all too keen to accept something undesirable
5	'… vague, swilling concepts' (line 26)	as if no one had any idea what was really going on or why it happened
6	'sessions of sorrow …digitised despair' (line 33)	alliteration to mock assumed importance
7	'the Diana moment turned into the George moment' (lines 44–45)	as if it can be/is being applied to nearly anyone

continued ➤

'Public Grief'

8	'media hearse rolling heedlessly downhill' (lines 45–46)	black humour in comparison of media to 'hearse' – especially in context
9	'If Sky News … then BBC News 24 …' (lines 50–52)	idea of false logic, no reason for coverage other than presence of competitor
10	'Call for … Kill … Order …' (lines 52–53)	echoing the peremptory tones of some bossy editor
11	'Kill a few more forests.' (lines 52–53)	newspapers reduced to the raw material they are made from
12	'Joe Public … and his kids' (lines 54–55)	fairly contemptuous, slang reference to the general public and their children
13	' – like a bit part in a reality TV show' (lines 55–56)	throwaway last line; 'bit part' suggests no importance; 'reality TV show' has connotations of poor quality, mass-appeal, tacky, …

4 **Use appropriate material from your answers to the preceding questions (and any other points you think are relevant) to write a structured response to one of the following exam-type questions:**

[Marking Instructions in the style of those for formal tests are given below, but if students have been given a good allocation of time (and this is desirable), it might be sensible to 'double' the marks.]

The mark for this question should reflect the overall quality of the response and may not be directly related to the length of the response or to the number of points/references made. A succinct, sophisticated response should be worth more than a series of fairly trivial points and obvious references. 'Ticking and adding up' is not appropriate (or fair) here.

For full marks there must be reference to both passages (although not necessarily a balanced treatment) and convincing evaluative comment. Where reference is made to one passage only, the maximum mark is 3 (6).

(a) **Which passage gives you a clearer picture of the influence of the media in manipulating 'public grief'? Justify your choice by referring to the ideas of both passages.**

Note that candidates are instructed to focus on ideas.

Key points are identified in suggested answers to 1, 2(a) and 3(a) above.

The following guidelines should be used:

5 marks (or 9/10 marks)	intelligent understanding of both passages; ability to compare/contrast relevant ideas is strong
4 marks (or 7/8 marks)	clear understanding of both passages; ability to compare/contrast relevant ideas is evident

continued ➤

'Public Grief'

---

3 marks (or 5/6 marks)	understanding of both passages; some ability to compare/contrast relevant ideas is discernible
2 marks (or 3/4 marks)	some understanding of both passages; limited ability to compare/contrast relevant ideas
1 mark (or 1/2 marks)	one or two relevant but unconvincing points

(b) Which writer's style do you find more effective in conveying her/his attitude to 'public' grief'? Justify your choice by referring to the style of both passages.

Note that candidates are instructed to focus on style.

Marking Guidelines for **style only** can be found with Set One (pages 7–8).

Key points are identified in suggested answers to 1, 2(b) and 3(b) above, although reference could be made in addition to:

- Grant's much more personal approach (prayer in church, …)

- Grant focuses almost exclusively on Bigley

- Preston's use of several examples (Best, Diana, Queen Mother, Pope John Paul II)

- Preston's less assertive style

Set Five
Terrible Teenagers

Choose any two of the passages and answer either of the following questions:

> *(a)* **Which passage do you think more effectively conveys the writer's views about the relationship between adults and teenagers? Justify your choice by detailed reference to the style of writing in each passage.**

Marking Guidelines for **style only** can be found with Set One (pages 7–8).

The following points could be made about **style**:

Passage One:

- generally an impassioned, highly rhetorical style; fairly 'preachy'

- structured round truancy case in England (though starts with generalised comments); moves to Scottish opinion; rounds off with reference to other countries' education systems

- question/answer opening – dramatic

- repetition of 'we need' (*passim*)

- effective illustration of authority figures ('the old bowler hat, the gaffer, the policeman, the dominie, the sergeant-major' + designed to sound old-fashioned)

- emotional references ('the Somme and the Holocaust')

- the direct address in 'Surely all this is obvious.'

- mocking use of 'Dickensian'

- the dramatic 'No – it is a disaster.'

- sarcasm, slight humour in stereotyping of 'bohemian, kaftan-wearing luvvies'

- hint of cliché in lines 30–34: 'pushing … into a corner', 'currency … devalued', 'another step on the road'

- the slightly self-mocking 'Thank goodness for devolution' followed by 'just in time to stop us getting smug'

- relatively straightforward style in lines 42–61

- rhetorical flourish in last paragraph: 'we need' (for 12th(?) time); political buzz words: 'empower … freedom … choice … co-operation'; imperatives 'Make … let'; imagery of 'lead the way'; monosyllabic nature of last sentence

continued ➤

Terrible Teenagers

Passage Two:

- generally, it could be argued, the style of this passage is uneven and not always suited to the task – perhaps a feature of the slightly contradictory nature of the line of thought (see below)

- structure: specific incident in Rochdale – general observations on 'teenagers today' – shift to recollection of own teenage days – return to Rochdale

- tone of opening? ostensibly factual, but Biblical echo of 'come to pass' suggests not wanting to be taken too seriously; odd choice of 'malevolent' …

- teenagers' casual/threatening attitude conveyed by 'loafing … smoking … swigging … chuck … thunder'

- description of parishioners a bit sardonic, 'folk', 'cower', 'fraying thoughts'

- upper case in 'Rampaging Teenager' – implies a kind of title given by others – seems to be distancing herself from the criticism

- list of activities in lines 16–18 makes teenagers sound very threatening

- appears to make concessionary point that there are many untroublesome teenagers (lines 19–22) but describes them very sarcastically ('the gleam of their teeth competing with the high sheen of their results')

- illustration from personal experience – attitude to teenagers revealed in language? e.g. 'gallumphing' is fairly unthreatening

- 'Teenagers now are awful, I think.' (line 34) – the addition of 'I think' is important – could be 'think' in sense of 'believe' or in sense of 'I'm not really sure'

- nostalgic tone of recollection in lines 35–46

- deliberate contrast of tone: 'killed … diverting little hoo-hah' (lines 45–46)

- lines 47–52 contain serious argument and are marked by an abrupt shift to very sophisticated vocabulary and structures

- conclusion attempts to bring together the point that most teenagers merely lack consideration with the point that adults have lost authority and bring it all back to Rochdale. Skilful or fumbled? Tone? – not entirely serious ('retake the church' is sort of mock heroic)

Passage Three:

- generally very relaxed, sympathetic, positive; fairly informal, personal

- introduction includes many examples, often listed to suggest extent of 'problem', variously integrated, by single dash, pair of dashes, colon

- repetition of 'love' to emphasise (unusual) attitude; repetition of 'I' to stress personal attachment/involvement

- mysterious/intriguing idea of 'half world' (line 15)

continued ➤

Terrible Teenagers

- effective structuring of 'They ..., but ...; they ..., but ...' (lines 17–19) to highlight contradictory nature of teenagers' situation

- contrast of 'energy' and 'tired' in lines 22–23 to support her approval of voting plan

- positive, sympathetic connotations of words such as 'altruistic, idealistic and determined'

- adoption of teenagers' 'voice' and structure in 'Wars are a crime against humanity – end of story.'

- positive, sympathetic connotations of words such as 'idealism ... fresh ... forthright ... passionate' (line 38)

- tone of 'old fogeys' (line 39)

- unaggressive tone of 'maybe' (line 41)

- imagery of 'well' (line 56) – implies deep, life-enhancing, ...

- vocabulary of the conclusion is more formal, elevated than rest ('potential ... integrate ... constituents ... afforded ... process ... alienated')

(b) Which writer's view of the way teenagers are (and should be) perceived by adults are you more inclined to agree with? Justify your choice by detailed reference to the ideas of both passages.

Marking Guidelines for **ideas only** can be found with Set Four (pages 18–19).

The following points could be made about **ideas**:

Passage One:

- not good if young people merely conform/accept authority

- their independence/creativity should be encouraged

- if they won't attend school, we should find out why

- punishment of their parents is not the answer

- in many such families, could make a bad situation worse

- teenagers in general widely perceived as threatening

- people want more severe punishments

- but young people are the carers and wealth-producers of the future

- the best education system is one which encourages independence of thought

Passage Two:

The line of thought in this passage might be seen as a little loose, perhaps even contradictory – certainly not as dogmatic as the headline implies.

- teenagers generally source of fear for older people

- press concentrate on bad side

- writer admits to being intimidated by teenagers

continued ➤

Terrible Teenagers

- recalls her teenage years/instances of 'bad behaviour'
- all adult figures in past seemed to be working together
- teenagers not so much bad as thoughtless/inconsiderate
- adults today need to stand up for themselves

Passage Three:

- teenagers mostly reported negatively
- writer states she actually likes them
- recognises their difficult situation
- applauds plan to extend franchise
- they have a genuine, if unsophisticated, interest in political matters
- they can spot the absurdities of adult rules
- they make a positive contribution to life
- they respond in kind to negative adult perceptions
- they should be treated with respect

Marking Guidelines for:
Close Reading Practice Papers

Introduction

The Marking Instructions for the six Practice Papers in Part Three of the pupil book follow the format and style of the Marking Instructions issued for past examinations.

The answers are extremely full and are trying to cover all possibilities. The nature of the 'open' questioning means that there will always be appropriate answers which are not recorded in these instructions. The emphasis, however, should be on 'appropriate'. When 'appropriate' comment is required, it must make some valid attempt to answer the question as asked. The comment might well be appropriate in a general sense, but it is the particular context that matters.

The use of lists and tables helps to make clear the constituents of good answers to the markers for assessment purposes. This is not necessarily a good approach to writing answers.

Much of the difficulty in assessing students' work arises from the distinction between a 'fully developed' answer – most often rewarded by two marks, and a 'basic' answer, typically rewarded by one mark. It takes only half a dozen errors by the marker on one side or the other of this balance to distort the overall assessment of a student's work. Most people can recognise a full 'correct' answer and have no hesitation in awarding two marks. More problematical is where the answer is 'correct' but not fully convincing; or the one which stumbles by tiny increments towards an answer which eventually demonstrates some understanding. For the purposes of this book and these exercises, erring on the side of caution could do the student more favours in the long run. By being constantly more demanding, markers can encourage further effort. It should be noted that 'further effort' does not necessarily mean writing longer answers. It really means thinking more effectively before producing an exact, penetrating (and sometimes shorter) answer.

Paper One

Teen Magazines

Passage One: Drooling Over Boys

Passage Two: Girl Power

Questions on Passage One

1   Read lines 1–19.

   (a) **What does the writer mean when she says the publishers of *Mad About Boys* were 'weeping into their spreadsheets'?**   **1 U**

They were upset at the (potential) loss of sales/income (i.e. an understanding of the implications of 'spreadsheet')

   (b) **Explain briefly what, according to lines 1–7, brought this about.**   **1 U**

There must be some attempt to use own words. Blatant lifts: 0.

because of the criticism/the actions of one big retailer/the adverse publicity

   (c) **Why, according to lines 8–19, is the writer inclined to agree with Dr Elliott's criticism?**   **2 U**

There must be some attempt to use own words. Blatant lifts: 0.

Marks will depend on the quality of explanation.

Possible answers:

   1   she refers to the girl on the cover as a 'child' while describing her adult appearance (2 marks)

   2   she believes 'the look' has sexual undertones (1 mark)

   3   she believes the magazines distort young girls' appearance (1 mark)

   4   she believes the magazines demean young girls (1 mark)

   (d) **How does the writer's word choice in lines 8–19 emphasise her disapproval of the magazine?**   **2 A**

Marks will depend on the quality of comment. Reference alone: 0. Candidates are free to deal with one or more than one example. An insightful comment on one example could score 2 marks; a more basic comment will be worth 1 mark.

Possible answers:

   1   'smirks'   suggests leering, provocative, …

   2   'strangely knowing'   suggests unnatural, corrupted, …   *continued* ➤

3	'numerous (boys)'	suggests promiscuity
4	'allegedly'	suggests duplicity, …
5	'hectic'	suggests uncontrolled, frenzied, chaotic, …
6	'hussies'	suggests brazen, immoral, …
7	'frisson'	suggests slightly dangerous, illicit thrill, …
8	'disturbing'	suggests disconcerting, unsettling, …

2 **Read lines 20–38.**

(a) **In what way do lines 20–22 act as a turning point in the writer's line of thought?   2 U**

Before this she has supported/agreed with the criticism of *MAB* (1); she is now going on to recognise/argue that there is an element of natural behaviour in what it represents (1).

An answer which treats the paragraph as a 'link' in the traditional way could score 2, provided it deals clearly with the change of attitude.

An answer which focuses on 'Yet' as an indicator of a 'turning point' could also score 2, provided it adequately contextualises the change. [Note that 'however' in line 20 is not relevant here.]

(b) **Referring closely to the language of lines 23–26, show how the writer pokes fun at herself.**   **2 A**

Marks will depend on the quality of comment. Reference alone: 0. An insightful comment on one example could score up to 2 marks; a more basic comment will be worth 1 mark. Note that 'pokes fun at herself' is in the question and that mere repetition of this will not deserve any credit.

Word choice will provide the most likely source of comment, but other aspects of 'language' could be explored.

Possible answers:

1	'(rather) plain'	bluntly denies any physical attractiveness
2	'skinny'	emphasises/exaggerates her thinness
3	'wistfully'	acknowledges rather hopeless yearning
4	'obsessed'	acknowledges almost irrational, fanatical preoccupation
5	'trappings'	realises trivial, ephemeral nature of fashion

continued ➢

6	'like a pipecleaner'	humorous comparison with something extremely thin
7	'flailing'	sense of exaggerated, hopeless desperation
8	'painstakingly'	emphasises the effort for little or no success
9	'scarlet'	extremely bright, aggressive colour to emphasise the absurdity of the outcome
10	the parenthetical ' – in a flailing, aspirational gesture'	provides dramatic pause after 'but' to delay the punchline about her toenails; and includes the climax of her self-criticism

(c) How effective do you find the anecdote in lines 27–31 in illustrating the writer's point in this paragraph?   **2 E**

Candidates are free to find the anecdote effective or not. Marks will depend on the quality of explanation and comment. Up to 2 marks for an acceptable explanation which refers sensibly to the ideas and/or language of the anecdote.

Mere paraphrase of the anecdote: 0.

Key point: the anecdote aims to show that when very young girls attempt to use cosmetics/fashion to their advantage, the result is (often) the opposite.

Effectiveness (or lack thereof) could be discussed in terms of the humour or the clarity with which the anecdote illustrates the point.

Supporting reference/comment could come from ideas or from language:

Ideas:

1   The main purpose of the earrings was to identify herself as a girl and this was subverted when the father's friend thought she was a boy.

Language:

2	'genial'	friendliness, warmth is ironic in contrast with the cruelty of the remark
3	'boomed'	to emphasise the embarrassment caused by the certainty of the speaker
4	placing of 'son'	as climax of anecdote, emphasises shock, embarrassment

(d) Show how the writer's attitude to today's 'retail industry' is made clear by her language in lines 32–38. Refer in your answer to more than one language feature.   **4 A**

Marks will depend on the quality of comment. Reference alone: 0. Mere identification of feature: 0. An insightful comment on one example/feature could score up to 3 marks; a more

continued ➤

> *Teen Magazines*

basic comment will be worth 1 mark. For full marks there must be reference to more than one language feature.

Possible answers:

Word choice:

1	'latched on'	suggests grasping, parasitical, predatory, …
2	'(glittering) tat'	suggests the merchandise, while superficially bright and attractive, is completely worthless
3	'nasty'	suggests they are cheap, offensive, …
4	'galloping spending power'/ 'avaricious little hearts'	it could be argued that these expressions suggest the way retailers have a stereotyped view of young people and exploit them accordingly

Sentence structure:

5	positioning of 'But'	clear indication of change in attitude
6	use of semi-colon	allows balance between 'then' and 'now'
7	positioning of 'Today'	emphasises focus on unsatisfactory state of affairs now
8	use of colon + list	to introduce/highlight the range of undesirable items

Tone:

9	'a thousand nasty shades'	contemptuous exaggeration
10	use of inverted commas round 'Tweenies'	presents it as an undignified term, suggesting contemptuous, exploitative attitude of the retailers who make use of it
11	any of 1–8 above	appropriate comment

3 *(a)* **Explain in your own words what, according to lines 39–54, the writer sees as the 'chief problem' about *Mad About Boys*.** **2 U**

There must be some attempt to use own words. Blatant lift: 0.

For full marks there should be an acceptable gloss of 'obsession with the opposite sex', e.g. fixation, mania, fascination, … + a gloss of either 'craven', e.g. cowardly, weak, unquestioning, … or 'relentless', e.g. unremitting, constant, never ceasing, …

Sensible reference to the 'older men' idea could score 1 mark.

Sensible reference to the use of the plural 'boys' should be rewarded.   *continued* ➤

Teen Magazines

(b) **Show how the writer's language creates a humorous tone in lines 44 ('Its readers. . .')–54.**   **2 A**

Marks will depend on the quality of comment. Reference alone: 0. An insightful comment on one example could score up to 2 marks; a more basic comment will be worth 1 mark.

Possible references/comments:

1	the headlines quoted	the cumulative banality of their subject matter (and patronisingly 'teenage' language – 'lads', 'gear', 'guy', 'boyf', repetition of 'sexy') ends up being funny
2	'presumably'	mock uncertainty
3	'grinning 15-year-old'	hints at caricature
4	'(go for the) older man'	use of 'adult' terminology is ironic when referring to 'little girls'; 15-year-old not exactly 'older man'
5	'oddly enough'	tongue-in-cheek, as if the producers of the magazine should have realised this
6	'exhausting'	as if in sympathy with the girls

4   **Read lines 55–64.**

(a) **Explain in your own words two problems the writer predicts for readers of *Mad About Boys* when they grow up.**   **2 U**

There must be some attempt to use own words. Blatant lifts: 0.

Any two of the following for 1 mark each:

1   they could find it hard to adjust to sensible (monogamous) relationships

2   they could become promiscuous

3   they could find it hard to become independent

(b) **Show how the writer uses sentence structure in these lines to highlight the problems.**   **2 A**

Marks will depend on the quality of comment. Mere identification of feature: 0. An insightful comment on one example could score up to 2 marks; a more basic comment will be worth 1 mark.

Possible answers:

1	use of a series of questions	illustrates idea of uncertainties, answers required, …
2	parenthetical '– drummed into her from an early age –'	reminds reader that the root of the problem has been established over a lengthy period

continued ➤

> ### Teen Magazines

3	'note,'	extra signpost for reader to draw attention to key point
4	list ('mad about …')	illustrates the extent of the uncertainty
5	repetition of 'mad about'	hints at being out of control, …
6	'Or …'	dramatic introduction of desirable (but unlikely?) resolution of the problems

5 *(a)* **Explain in your own words the 'paradox' to which the writer refers in line 65.**   **2 U**

There must be some attempt to use own words. Blatant lifts: 0.

1 mark for each of the following:

when women relied on men financially, girls' magazines dealt with/encouraged useful/practical activities

now women are more independent, girls' magazines represent them as passive creatures/interested only in boys

   (b) **How effective do you find the last paragraph (lines 65–69) as a conclusion to the passage as a whole? Refer in your answer to the ideas and/or language of the paragraph.**   **3 E**

Marks will depend on the quality of comment on the ideas and/or language of the final paragraph. For full marks there must be some acceptable link to 'the passage as a whole'.

Comment could be on:

1   the effectiveness of the criticism of magazines/publishers

2   the tone of regret, sadness at the 'paradox'

3   the humour of 'knock together a handy cupboard'

4   the emptiness of 'nothing more'

5   the contrast between the variety in the past and the narrowness now

6   the contempt in 'drooling'

7   reference back to title/headline in final words

> Teen Magazines

Questions on Passage Two

6   *(a)*   **What, according to the opening sentence, did 'Girl Power' seem to offer?**   **1 U**

Acceptable gloss on '(rhetoric of) choice, control and empowerment' for 1 mark (Blatant lift: 0.)

E.g. taking charge, not being told what to do, having options, being the boss,…

   (b)   **Why, according to the writer in the rest of the first paragraph, is it 'difficult to gauge its real impact?' (lines 3–4)**   **2 U**

Any of the following for up to 2 marks, depending on the quality of explanation. Blatant lifts: 0.

    1   gloss on 'construct a fanfare around a ripple' e.g. commentators are always liable to exaggerate the future influence of a current phenomenon which may in fact be of minimal importance

    2   it is too early: only when those who were young when 'Girl Power' arose have grown up will we know what influence it had

    3   currently, the only signs of its effects suggest no radical changes or merely support the conventional picture of women's role/status

7   *(a)*   **How does the context of lines 11–17 help you to understand the expression 'no images of empowerment'? (lines 13–14)**   **2 U**

1 mark for acceptable meaning + 1 mark for successful link to context. Note that where meaning is not acceptable, there is no mark for a reference to context which would otherwise be acceptable.

Meaning: no (suggestions of) taking control, or being given independence, or being treated equally, …

Context: all the activities referred to ('boys … looking good … fill in the time … dating boys … make-up' etc.) are trivial, passive, …

   (b)   **Referring closely to the language of lines 18–29, show how the writer makes clear her contempt for the magazines she describes.**   **4 A**

Marks will depend on the quality of comment. Reference alone: 0. Mere identification of feature: 0. An insightful comment on one example/feature could score up to 3 marks; a more basic comment will be worth 1 mark.

Possible answers:

1	'limited to'	suggests narrowness, inadequacy of content
2	'total elision'	points out the complete avoidance, with hint of deliberate evasion
3	'pure (teen focus)'	emphasises the exclusive, narrow outlook of the content

continued ➤

> *Teen Magazines*

4	'claims to be'	suggestion of spurious self-promotion
5	list of typical content areas	highlights the range of relatively trivial issues dealt with
6	'disingenuously'	suggestion of deception, deviousness, …
7	'snogging'	placed inside inverted commas draws attention to inappropriateness of the term for serious idea contained in 'relationships'
8	choice of quoted headlines/extracts	cumulatively create impression of trivial outlook

8   **Read lines 30–39.**

Explain in your own words the writer's key criticism of the way the magazines deal with:

(a)   **girls' place in society;**   **2 U**

Up to 2 marks for an explanation of 'offer little support to the ideals of self-determination and autonomy, setting much greater store on fitting within society's ideal'. Blatant lifts: 0.

Key areas:

'ideals of self-determination and autonomy' – (aspiration to) independence

'fitting within society's ideal' – conforming, not being different, …

(b)   **girls' attitudes to boys.**   **1 U**

Gloss on 'one long scramble to get a "lush lad"' – boys are merely the object of the chase for a (desirable) boyfriend

9   **Consider the last paragraph of the passage (lines 40–49).**

(a)   **What, in your opinion, is the tone of this paragraph?**   **1 A**

serious, didactic, pessimistic, gloomy, depressed, negative, …

(b)   **Explain in detail how this tone is created.**   **3 A**

Marks will depend on the quality of comment. Reference alone: 0. Mere identification of a feature: 0. An insightful comment on one example/feature could score up to 3 marks; a more basic comment will be worth 1 mark.

Possible answers, depending on tone identified:

1   extensive use of formal language ('doyenne', 'misogyny', 'vistas of anxiety', 'conceptually naïve', 'trade on a sense of lack', …

2   agreeing with Greer's very negative assertion ('misogyny', 'hopelessness') sets similarly negative tone

continued ➤

> *Teen Magazines*

3   'All [they] seem to do …' suggests the very limited ambitions/effectiveness of the magazines

4   'glossy' – rather contemptuous word, pointing out the superficiality of the magazines

5   'further vistas of anxiety' – contrast of hope implied by 'vistas' with fears, criticism contained in 'anxiety'

6   list ('one's body, one's boyfriend, one's lifestyle, one's attitude') highlights the range of worries created by the magazines

7   'need to trade on a sense of lack' suggests exploitative nature of the magazines' approach to readers in order to satisfy advertisers

8   'never extend beyond' highlights the limitations, lack of aspiration encouraged by the magazines

9   'No wonder' – rather colloquial, resigned tone of acceptance

10   'lack of self-esteem or ambition' – absence of two such vital qualities is deeply worrying

11   'epidemic' – comparison with widespread illness

Question on both Passages

10   **Which passage, in your opinion, more effectively explores the shortcomings of teenage girls' magazines?**

Justify your choice by referring closely to the style of writing of both passages.   5 A/E

Note that candidates are instructed to focus on style. Reference to the ideas of the passages is, of course, unavoidable and will in many cases strengthen the candidate's response.

The mark for this question should reflect the overall quality of the response and may not be directly related to the length of the response or to the number of points/references made. A succinct, sophisticated response should be worth more than a series of fairly trivial points and obvious references. 'Ticking and adding up' is not appropriate (or fair) here.

For full marks there must be reference to both passages (although not necessarily a balanced treatment) and convincing evaluative comment. Where reference is made to one passage only, the maximum mark is 3.

The following guidelines should be used:

5 marks   clear and intelligent understanding of style in both passages; effective references; evaluative comment is convincing

continued ➤

Teen Magazines

4 marks   clear understanding of style in both passages; sensible references; evaluative comment is reasonably convincing

3 marks   understanding of style in both passages; adequate references; discernible evaluative comment

2 marks   some understanding of style; limited reference; at least one appropriate evaluative comment

1 mark   one or two relevant but unconvincing comments

The following points could be made, but all points which candidates propose will have to be judged on their merits:

Passage One:

predominantly colloquial style:	'weeping into their spreadsheets'
	'is up there with'
	'caking themselves'
	'tramping around'
	'galloping spending power'
	'tat'
use of personal anecdote:	toenail painting
	earrings and father's friend
	brother's gift
use of cultural references:	range of films mentioned in paragraph 3
	Mary Poppins
sarcastic tone	lines 39–64

Passage Two:

predominantly formal, academic style, with hint of sociological jargon:	'rhetoric of choice, control and empowerment'
	'reassertion of traditional models'
	'filtered into the teen consciousness'

continued ➤

Teen Magazines

	'images of empowerment'
	'logical extension'
	'non-conformity'
	'self-determination and autonomy'
	'self-esteem'
reference to feminist icon	Germaine Greer
pessimistic tone	lines 40–49

Paper Two

Fight to Save Our Food

Passage One: The Fight to Save Our Food

Passage Two: 'I'm Lovin' It'

Questions on Passage One

1   **'Modern food policies are screwing up the world.' (line 1)**

    What are the consequences of modern food policies, according to the writer? You should answer in your own words.   **3 U**

    There must be some attempt to use own words. Blatant lifts: 0.

    Any three of the following for 1 mark each:

    1   people are dying

    2   preventing the continuance of cooking particular to each culture/family

    3   agricultural survival (and its attendant lifestyle) becomes financially impossible

    4   animal cruelty in farming is increasing

2   **Show how the writer's tone in lines 7–9 is made clear by the language he uses.**   **2 A**

    Up to 2 marks are available for the identification of an appropriate tone with a reference to the text and an explanation as to how the reference links to the tone. Mere identification of an appropriate tone without any reference or explanation: 0. Reference alone: 0.

    Tone: sceptical, ironic, disbelieving or other appropriate tone

1	'Yet'	suggests that what follows beggars belief
2	'supposed to' (accept and admire)	suggests they are not laudable/credible
3	'they claim'	suggests claim is not a fact
4	inverted commas round 'progress'	denies that the change is actually advancing anything good
5	'despoliation' versus 'progress'	contrasts the actual destruction they cause with their barefaced claim they are making things better

> Fight to Save Our Food

3   **Read lines 10–29.**

(a) **What are the two major points the writer makes in lines 15–29 about how the 'leaders have got it all horribly wrong'? (line 12)**   **2 U**

There must be some attempt to use own words. Blatant lifts: 0.

hunger and inequality are rife. (1)

big global corporations run the food industry for their own benefit. (1)

(b) **How do sentence structure and word choice in lines 10–29 persuade the reader to adopt his point of view?**   **4 A**

Marks will depend on the quality of comment. Reference alone: 0. An insightful comment on one example could gain up to 3 marks; a more basic comment will be worth 1 mark. Both sentence structure and word choice have to be dealt with to gain full marks.

Sentence structure:

1	'There's already…' short sentence	confident declarative statement – convincing in its directness
2	dash (line 11)	introduces the uncomfortable truth which has to be faced
3	parenthesis (line 12)	insists we must agree with his point
4	dash (line 13)	signals the expansion of 'first principles' – basic questions follow
5	repetition of 'and' in list of clauses (lines 13–14)	stresses that there are a number of imperative questions we have to ask
6	question sentence (line 15)	rhetorical device to introduce his reasons to follow
7	'Not at all' (line 15)	simple trenchant phrase reinforces his defence, answers his question to convince the reader definitively of his view
8	'But' (line 17)	introduces a flat contradiction to the positive points about food made before
9	parenthesis (line 18)	adds an even more alarming statement to his argument
10	'Yet' (line 19)	suggests an extreme contrast – here, the existence of obesity beside the hunger

continued ➢

> *Fight to Save Our Food*

11	'not...but' (lines 26–7)	establishes the contrast between the expected humanitarian motive and the real cynical one

Word choice:

12	'(grasp the) nettle'	face up to the problem one is reluctant to tackle but which one might overcome in the same way as one does by gripping a nettle boldly to stop it stinging
13	'bedrock points'	connotations of elemental, immovable, fundamental starting point for all argument
14	'abundant'	connotations of plenty, overflowing quantities
15	'nutritious'	connotations of goodness, nurturing, creating well being
16	'gross obesity'	extreme connotations of 'gross' – both size and a hint of disgust
17	'ponderous globe (of a child)'	suggests the immense weight and rotund shape of the child
18	'fruits'	connotations of a desirable nutritious product, here, ironically, the corrupt result
19	'sacrificed'	connotations of giving something up for the greater good – here, thrown away for an unworthy cause

4   **Read lines 30–44.**

(a) **Comment on the impact and function of lines 30–31 in the development of his argument.**   **2 A**

One mark available for impact; one mark available for function.

Impact:

impact is created by the use of a single sentence paragraph standing on its own, claiming to be self-evident, drawing attention to itself as an important statement (1)

or

use of 'And' at the beginning of the sentence highlights the idea that here is an important addition to the statement he has made earlier (1)

or

use of 'ingredients' is both appropriate in meaning and acts as a topic sentence (1)

Function:

links the idea of profit from the previous paragraph with the three ingredients which are to follow in the next paragraphs (1)

Fight to Save Our Food

(b) Explain what, according to the writer, is the disadvantage of each of the 'ingredients of profit'.　　　　　**3 U**

There should be some attempt to recast in own words. Blatant lifts: 0.

1　huge production causes an excess of farming products (1)

2　cutting costs means employing many fewer people on the land (1)

3　'adding value' can lead to adulteration of original real products (1)

5　Read lines 45–51.

(a) Explain why globalisation makes the situation worse.　　　　　**2 U**

There should be some attempt to recast in own words.

Any 2 of the following for 1 mark each:

1　farmers are in fierce competition with each other

2　increased mechanisation cuts labour

3　some poor farmers work for big corporations on the corporations' very unrewarding terms

4　big supermarkets buy from the cheapest in the world thus increasing the cut throat competition/exploiting the producer

(b) How does the writer's word choice in these lines accentuate the idea that globalisation is detrimental to farming?　　　　　**2 A**

Marks will depend on the quality of comment. Reference alone: 0. An insightful comment on one example could gain more than 1 mark; a more basic comment will be worth 1 mark.

1	'(global) dogfight'	suggests a bitter/demeaning struggle (to sell products)
2	'modern imperialism'	suggests the exploitation of disadvantaged people (like third world farmers)
3	'slave wages'	highlights the very low level of rewards – almost working hard for nothing as the slaves did
4	'(make a) virtue'	pretending underhand methods are actually praiseworthy – suggests globalisation is exploitative
5	'desperate (farmers)'	shows the extreme conditions they have to cope with

Fight to Save Our Food

6   **Read lines 52–60.**

(a) **Briefly state the writer's solution to the problems identified in the previous paragraph. 1 U**

There should be some attempt to recast in own words.

agricultural practices have to be grounded in good biology (sustainable in the world as a whole) (1)

or

establish how much food is required and how to produce it (1)

(b) **Show how sentence structure in these lines helps to support his argument.**   **2 A**

Marks will depend on the quality of comment. Reference alone: 0. An insightful comment on one feature could gain more than 1 mark; a more basic comment will be worth 1 mark.

1	two short sentence(s) (line 52)	one points despairingly back to problems; the second optimistically looks forward
2	either short sentence (line 52)	direct, matter-of-fact tone instilling confidence in his argument
3	series of three 'and's	to build up the scale and/or surprising number of conflicting ideals
4	dash followed by 'but' (line 54)	provides emphasis on what needs to be done if these things are to be achieved
5	dash (line 56)	introduces the addition of a definition of 'sound biology'
6	list after dash (lines 56–57)	range of biologies climaxing in 'the world as a whole'
7	balance in sentence 'just as…so'	defines a methodology which reinforces his claims
8	'Then we need…' (line 59)	concludes with the important practical instruction in a simple statement

7   **'… enlightened agriculture reflects nature.' (line 61)**

Using your own words as far as possible, give any three examples of this which are described in lines 61–69.   **3 U**

There must be some attempt to use own words. Blatant lifts: 0.

Each of the following for 1 mark:

1   appropriate good land should be used for growing the crops which provide the basic foods like bread and cereals (1)

2   really fertile land should be saved for the growing of fruit and vegetables (1)

3   poorer land on hills or land which is too wet for crops should be used for rearing animals for meat (1)

> *Fight to Save Our Food*

8 **Show how the word choice or tone of lines 70–74 emphasises the writer's criticism of present day farming.** **2 A**

Marks will depend on the quality of comment. Reference alone: 0. An insightful comment on one example of word choice could gain 2 marks; a more basic comment will be worth 1 mark. Identification of an appropriate tone justified by a reference and comment could gain 2 marks. Mere identification of tone: 0.

Word choice:

1   'global'   suggests enormous and unaccountable scale – planet sized

2   'massive'   suggests excessive size

3   'maximise'   concentration on large quantities (at all costs)

4   'incredible'   almost impossible to accept

5   'vast (scale)'   suggests inconceivable size (and range)

6   'competitors'   animals no longer a source of food but taking the food out of human mouths

Tone:

7   reference to any of the items included in word choice with a related comment linking it to an appropriate tone

8   reference to climactic nature of sentence structure 'Half the…' with comment linking to an appropriate tone

9   reference to use of statistics in support of argument linked to an appropriate tone

10 reference to alliterative quality of 'pursuit of profit' / 'maximise meat' with comment linking to an appropriate tone

Appropriate tones might include: angry, emotive, critical, argumentative…

9 **Read lines 75–87.**

What course of action does the writer recommend in these lines and what does he hope might be a consequence of this action? **2 U**

There must be some attempt to use own words. Blatant lifts: 0.

we as consumers have to make an effort to seek out better food sources (1)

and either

the expensive prices for real food might come down (1)

or

our pressure might persuade governments and supermarkets' organisations to change their ways (1)

Fight to Save Our Food

Questions on Passage Two

10   Read lines 1–10.

(a) **In your own words explain the writer's definition of a fantasy headline. (lines 1–3)   2 U**

gloss on 'the announcement of events…significance' – statement of something important and unusual (1)

gloss on 'chime irresistibly…ambitions' – fits in exactly with an individual's beliefs and/or hopes (1)

(b) **Show how the language of lines 3–10 highlights his appreciation of the fantasy headline mentioned in lines 3–4. You should consider more than one technique in your answer. 4 A**

Marks will depend on the quality of comment. Reference alone: 0. An insightful comment on one example could gain up to 3 marks; a more basic comment will be worth 1 mark. Two techniques have to be dealt with for full marks.

Word choice:

1	'loathing'	suggests a really strong hatred/now satisfied
2	'air-punching (moment)'	suggests the (physical) expression of his great joy
3	'(daze of) delighted disbelief'	an extreme expression of his happy feelings/fantasy realised
4	'shouting'	merely saying is not enough – his expression has to be loud and emphatic
5	'clenched (teeth and/or fists)'	strong physical reaction to emphasize his strong feelings
6	'primordial stuff'	strong primitive human emotion
7	'(greater) the glee'	a strong expression of happiness (with a smug self-justification)

Imagery:

Answers on imagery must 'deconstruct' the image, i.e. show an understanding of the literal root of the image and then explore how the writer is extending it figuratively.

8	'(bigger) the beast that's fallen'	he takes delight in the fact that the corporation which has had a setback is one of the biggest of its kind – like the king animal at the top of the chain

Sentence structure:

9	'Yes!' (line 4)	single word exclamatory sentence emphasises the degree of his agreement with the headline

continued ➢

Fight to Save Our Food

10	'And when I'd done...' (line 6)	'And' at the beginning of the sentence helps to show that the delight is just sinking in and he has to show it again in another way
11	repetition of 'YES!' or capitalisation and exclamation mark	emphasises the extent of his feelings at realising a longed for event
12	repetition of 'clenched'	gives further weight to his strong physical reaction of joy
13	'And the bigger the...' (line 9)	'And' at the beginning of the sentence helps to show that the new thought of the size or importance of the event has sprung to mind as another reason for joy
14	'the bigger...the greater' (lines 9–10)	use of comparatives conveys the correspondingly escalating scale of the responses
15	short final sentence	gives impact to his final (exclamatory) simple statement of his delight (and mirrors/repeats the headline to hammer home his feelings)/ ironically quotes a well-known catch phrase

16 Alliteration:

Several examples could be chosen, but the reference to alliteration alone would be worth nothing without an associated comment such as the ones on word choice above.

17 Other features such as the use of colloquial language or shifts in register or tone could be chosen and should be treated on their merits.

11 How does sentence structure in lines 11–24 emphasise the variety and quality of the takeaway sector?
2 A

Marks will depend on the quality of comment. Reference alone: 0. An insightful comment on a feature of sentence structure could gain more than 1 mark; a more basic comment will be worth 1 mark.

1	dash – 'far from it' (line 11)	the brief monosyllabic phrase intensifies the preceding statement
2	'But as...diversifying' (line 12)	balanced sentence introduces both elements of his contention – the size and the variety
3	the listing of the 'genuine alternatives' after the colon in line 15	the number of outlets mentioned gives the impression of an endless stream of different kinds of attractive, healthy outlets

continued ➤

Fight to Save Our Food

4	the dash (line 17) and the following statement	saves the most promising (organic or unlikely) outlet to the last, thus creating an effective climax
5	the use of inverted commas round 'real food'	serves to distinguish between the food he prefers and the food offered by the big chains which he implies is 'not real food'
6	'not only...but transparency ... ingredients' (lines 23–24)	list of three items after 'not only... but' lends importance to the final elements he sees as desirable in the new type of fast foods/stresses the equally important factor of easily tracing the origin of food

12   Read lines 25–35.

Why is the sentence 'The real stranglehold...big supermarkets' (lines 29–30) important in the structure of the argument of the passage?   **2 U**

It moves the subject on from the discussion on fast food (1)

to a discussion of the problems associated with big supermarkets (1)

13   Read lines 36–45.

In what ways do the writer's structure and punctuation clarify his attitude to supermarkets?   **4 A**

Marks will depend on the quality of comment. Reference alone: 0. An insightful comment on one example could gain up to 3 marks; a more basic comment will be worth 1 mark. In some answers there may be overlap between the two techniques. Answers which fall into this category should be treated sympathetically.

1	'For me, then, ...' (commas within this phrase)	the placing of 'For me' right at the beginning (isolated by the commas) shows that it is his own individual view
2	colon (line 37)	to introduce what the consumers should say
3	use of semi colons (lines 38–40)	separates each item in the list of commands to give each point a peremptory emphasis and clarity
4	repetition of 'enough of'	clarifies the idea of dictating to the supermarkets – stop these dubious practices
5	'enough of your dirty...miles'	climactic list conveys his abhorrence of the practices, particularly the last item, emphasised by three adjectives – the triad of condemnation!

continued ➤

> *Fight to Save Our Food*

6	repetition of 'you' (lines 41–45)	personalises his argument and lays the onus on the reader to do something
7	list of advice (lines 41–45)	covers/parallels the same areas as the previous list but gives the ethical alternatives
8	'And go...rest' (line 44)	full stop before 'And' highlights the blunt incontrovertible advice to avoid supermarkets

14 How appropriate is the final paragraph (lines 46–47) in the context of the whole passage?   1 E

it brings the article to a full circle with the idea of fantasy headlines (1)

or

fantasy headlines are applied to supermarkets at the end whereas at the beginning they were applied to fast food giants (1)

Questions on both Passages

15 Read lines 30–87 of Passage One and lines 25–47 of Passage Two.

Which writer is more effective in giving you an idea of the power exercised by supermarkets and the chances of that power being diminished by the public?

Justify your choice by referring to the ideas and style of both passages. You may wish to consider such stylistic aspects as structure, word choice, tone, imagery...   5 E

Note that candidates must deal with ideas **and** style.

Note: Ignore any reference to material outside the specified lines.

The mark for this question should reflect the overall quality of the response and may not be directly related to the length of the response or to the number of points/references made. A succinct, sophisticated response should be worth more than a series of fairly trivial points and obvious references. 'Ticking and adding up' is not appropriate (or fair) here.

For full marks there must be reference to both passages (although not necessarily a balanced treatment) and convincing evaluative comment. Where reference is made to one passage only, the maximum mark is 3.

The following guidelines should be used:

5 marks   clear and intelligent understanding of ideas and style in both passages; effective references; evaluative comment is convincing

4 marks   clear understanding of ideas and style in both passages; sensible references; evaluative comment is reasonably convincing

3 marks   understanding of ideas and style in both passages; adequate references; discernible evaluative comment

continued ➤

Fight to Save Our Food

2 marks   some understanding of ideas and/or style; limited reference; at least one
           appropriate evaluative comment

1 mark   one or two relevant but unconvincing comments

Ideas:

Passage One:

Cheap food is not really cheap; farmers are exploited because of the focus on cheapness; supermarkets' concentration on plentiful (and therefore cheap) meat skews the agricultural provision; common sense says this is not sustainable; if people go for 'better' more sustainable food it will become cheaper; the supermarkets will have to change.

Passage Two:

Supermarkets control bulk of food sales; monopoly position; many evils caused by monopoly – exploiting farmers, harming animals/human diet/the environment; a switch to ethical trading/shopping would cut the supermarkets' power.

Style:

Passage One:

scientific vocabulary	'agrarian economies', 'sound biology', 'staples', 'ruminants'…
down-to-earth vocabulary	'screwing up', 'pay for filler', 'caboodle', 'we can fix'…
use of statistics	line 18, lines 35–37, lines 72–73
argumentative structure	'yet'/'but'/'well'/'for'…
persuasive tone	'Yet we are supposed to…' 'Do I exaggerate? Not at all …'
effective last sentence	'The game's not over yet – but…'
simple sentences to make important points	

Passage Two:

personal viewpoint	'For me', 'I might just…' etc.
vivid imagery	'forays', 'liberate', 'corporate beasts', 'behemoth'
use of climax	line 40
direct address	lines 41–45
rhetorical structure	listing, balance, repetition ('yes', 'clenched', 'enough of…')
impact of last paragraph	

Paper Three

The Generation Gap

Passage One: 'Weirdness Dust' No More

Passage Two: The War of the Generations May Soon Be Over

Questions on Passage One

1 **Read lines 1–20.**

(a) **According to the writer, what change has taken place in young people's attitude to staying at home? Answer briefly and in your own words.** **1 U**

There must be some attempt to use own words. Blatant lifts: 0.

For the mark all that is required is a basic understanding that in the past staying at home was considered strange, an admission of failure, done only by 'losers' etc.; whereas now it is considered normal, ok, desirable, fashionable, not uncool…

Accept a simple statement such as 'Young people have a more positive attitude to staying at home' or 'They are less against it.'

(b) **Show how aspects of the writer's sentence structure highlight the idea of change.** **2 A**

Marks will depend on the quality of comment. Mere identification of feature: 0. Candidates must deal with more than one example.

Possible answers:

1	repetition of 'Time was'	highlights past, with implication of difference in present
2	short sentence 'Time was.'	abruptness hints that past attitude may have changed
3	repetition/parallelism of 'Time was. Time is …'	bluntly draws attention to the change
4	the comma after 'Time is'	allows pause which helps to heighten the contrast with 'Time was'
5	placing of 'Today'	draws attention to coming description of present attitude

> ## The Generation Gap

(c) 'Today it's perfectly cool to be in your twenties and still living with mum and dad.' (line 14)

How appropriate do you find the language of this sentence in the context of the writer's argument? **2 A/E**

Comment should be on the informality/colloquialism of 'cool' and/or 'your' and/or 'mum and dad'. Marks will depend on the quality of comment. Mere identification of the register: 0. A single insightful comment could score 2 marks; a more basic comment will be worth 1 mark.

Possible answers:

1   it is appropriate because she is talking about young people whose language this is

2   it is appropriate because it establishes a relaxed tone in line with the good relationships between the generations

3   it is inappropriate because it clashes with the more formal tone elsewhere

4   it is inappropriate because it is rather patronising for an adult writer to use 'teenage' language

2   Read lines 21–27.

(a) **Explain in your own words why the writer is so pleased at the results of the survey. 2 U**

There must be some attempt to use own words. Blatant lifts: 0.

For 2 marks, an answer should cover both of the following:

1   surveys typically produce findings which are disturbing, pessimistic, …

2   this one reveals a picture which is pleasing, agreeable, …

(b) **Show how the writer's imagery in the final sentence of the paragraph reinforces her point of view.** **2 A**

Marks will depend on the quality of comment. Candidates may refer to one or more than one image. An insightful comment on one image could be worth up to 2 marks; a weaker comment will be worth up to 1 mark.

Mere identification of the image: 0.

Answers on imagery must 'deconstruct' the image, i.e. show an understanding of the literal root of the image and then explore how the writer is extending it figuratively.

Possible answers:

1	'sign'	just as a sign gives important, helpful information, so the writer sees the findings of the survey as giving a clear indication of improving relations between the generations

continued ➤

The Generation Gap

2	'bedrock (of human life)'	just as bedrock is the solid rock underneath superficial formations, so the writer sees the family as a solid, supporting, unshakeable element in life
3	'unit'	just as a unit is a single entity, so the writer sees the family as a close-knit group
4	'warmth'	just as warmth/heat is essential to comfortable living, so the writer sees the family as something which helps sustains life
5	'cohesion'	just as cohesion involves sticking together, so the writer sees the family as something which holds people together socially

3 **Referring to lines 28–44, explain in your own words as far as possible the key differences the writer claims there are between parents now and parents from the previous generation.** **4 U**

There must be some attempt to use own words. Blatant lifts: 0.

A maximum of two points from each of the following lists for 1 mark each:

In the past:

1   fathers badly affected by war

2   unable to show love for children

3   enforced rules harshly

4   presided over unhappy homes which children were eager to leave

5   viewed child-rearing as an obligation, an unpleasant chore…

Now:

6   there are fewer bad parents

7   they show love to their children

8   they provide caring homes which children don't need/want to leave

4 **Why, according to the writer in the lines 45–49, have different generations 'never needed each other more'?** **2 U**

There must be some attempt to use own words. Blatant lifts: 0.

Any 2 of the following for one mark each:

1   modern life is in a state of change

continued ➤

> *The Generation Gap*

2   gloss on 'contradictory', e.g. full of inconsistency, paradoxical, ...

3   gloss on 'supple', e.g. modern life is flexible, uncertain, ...

4   gloss on 'unstructured', e.g. lacking fixed pattern, shapeless, ...

5   gloss on 'nothing lasts for long', e.g. there is little/no permanency

6   gloss on 'old boundaries have disappeared', e.g. former restrictions, limits have vanished

---

Questions on Passage Two

5   **Read lines 1–18.**

(a) **Explain in your own words what used to be society's attitude to young people who continued to stay in the parental home.**   **2 U**

There must be some attempt to use own words. Blatant lifts: 0.

An acceptable gloss of 'the pathetic compromise of the socially stunted' for 2 marks.

E.g.: it was a second-rate choice (1) made by people who couldn't cope on their own, were not developing socially as they should (1).

(b) **To what extent does the writer feel the term 'lifelong parenting' is an appropriate one?**   **2 U/E**

There must be some attempt to use own words. Blatant lifts: 0.

For full marks there must be some recognition of her uncertainty.

inappropriate in that it is hardly for the whole of life (1)

appropriate in that parents still giving money to those who have left home (1)

(c) **How effective do you find the writer's use of imagery in lines 13 ('But I do...')–18 in conveying her point of view?**   **4 A/E**

Marks will depend on the quality of comment. An insightful and developed comment, for example, on the extended metaphor in point 2 below, could score 3 or even 4 marks. More basic comments will be worth up to 1 mark. Mere identification of an image: 0.

Answers on imagery must 'deconstruct' the image; i.e. acknowledge the literal root and then show how the writer is extending this figuratively.

Possible answers:

1	'fragmenting ... consolidating'	uses notion of breaking into small pieces to describe the way the family is (alleged to be) breaking apart; then contrasts this with the notion of joining together to suggest there is a growing cohesion

continued ➤

> *The Generation Gap*

2	'toxic trench ... sliding into ... filled in'	(extended metaphor) describes ill-feeling within families as a deep pit of noxious material, then contrasts the idea of our moving unstoppably into this with the notion that it is now being done away with – idea of reconciliation ...; alternatively the trench could be seen as something which causes separation...

6   According to the writer in lines 19–25:

(a) **What does the term 'generation gap' mean?**   **1 U**

There must be some attempt to use own words. Blatant lifts: 0.

Acceptable gloss on 'a world with entirely different rules and morals' for 1 mark, e.g. parents and children have different/conflicting values, principles, outlooks, ...

Accept reference to a lack of understanding between the generations.

(b) **What are its effects?**   **2 U**

There must be some attempt to use own words. Blatant lifts: 0.

For full marks, answers should cover both of the following or provide a very good explanation of either:

1   gloss on 'irreparably alienated' – e.g. separated, unable to communicate, in a way that cannot be resolved

2   gloss on 'reach only the most fragile of compromises' – e.g. have only the slightest, flimsiest common ground

7   Read lines 26–37.

(a) **How effective do you find the writer's word choice in lines 26–27 in conveying her point of view about the generation gap?**   **2 A/E**

Marks will depend on the quality of comment. An insightful and developed comment on one word could score up to 2 marks. More basic comments will be worth up to 1 mark. Reference alone: 0.

Possible answers:

1	'clashes'	suggestion of violent confrontation, ...
2	'battles'	suggestion of hostility, fighting, violence, ...
3	'against'	suggestion of disagreement, conflict...
4	'deep-rooted'	suggestion that the problem has underlying causes greater than might appear, ...

(b) **Explain how the context of lines 32–37 makes clear the meaning of the expression 'seismic shifts'. (line 30)** **2 U**

Meaning: (change, movement) on a huge, massive scale.

Context: reference to and brief explanation of either of the following:

1   2% to 75% is an enormous rise, from virtually zero to three-quarters

2   parents, who in the past disapproved strongly of cohabitation, now may not only accept it but actually approve of it/see the advantages

(c) **How effective do you find the last sentence of lines 32–37 as a conclusion to the paragraph?** **2 E**

Marks will depend on the quality of comment/explanation. An insightful and developed explanation/comment could score up to 2 marks. More basic comments/explanations will be worth up to 1 mark. Mere paraphrase of the sentence: 0.

Possible answers:

1   it underlines the 'seismic shift' by taking the current parental attitude a stage beyond acceptance to one of positive approval

2   use of 'In fact …' to highlight the strangeness of this situation

3   use of colloquial 'don't much like' perhaps reflects more relaxed relationships

4   placing of 'blessing' at end of sentence underscores the positive attitude

5   element of humour in the irony lightens the tone

8   **Read lines 38–51.**

(a) **Show how the writer's language in lines 38–44 conveys the strength of her parents' reaction to her living with her boyfriend.** **2 A**

Marks will depend on the quality of comment. An insightful and developed comment on one word or feature could score up to 2 marks. More basic comments will be worth up to 1 mark. Reference alone: 0.

Possible answers:

Word choice:

1	'devastated'	suggests total shock, distress, world being shattered, …
2	'quite impossible'	suggests rigidity, certainty of parental outlook
3	'judged'	suggests (strong) moral stance

continued ➤

> The Generation Gap

4	'quite convinced'	suggests rigidity, certainty of parental outlook
5	'evil influence'	suggests judgement of boyfriend as dangerous, morally unsuitable, …
6	'(dangerously) deluded'	suggests extreme judgement of daughter as being duped, misled, …
7	'determined'	suggests rigidity, certainty of parental outlook

Sentence structure:

8	placing of 'devastated'	emphatic at end of sentence
9	repetition of 'dangerously deluded'	emphasises the conflict between the generations

(b) Show how the writer's language in lines 45–51 conveys her awareness of her own foolishness.   **2 A**

Marks will depend on the quality of comment. An insightful and developed comment on one word or feature could score up to 2 marks. More basic comments will be worth up to 1 mark. Reference alone: 0.

Possible answers:

Word choice:

1	'particularly difficult'	recognises not just a problem teenager but an especially trying one
2	'Crammed'	suggests that she is full to overflowing with stupid ideas
3	'daft'	blunt description, not just silly, but stupid, …
4	'unshakeable'	suggests rigidity of her beliefs
5	'invulnerability'	suggests superhuman, immortal, …
6	'dozen'	exaggeration
7	'idiotic'	blunt description of the choices as not merely silly but extremely unwise
8	'lunatic'	extreme description of the decision as not merely silly but unhinged
9	'capriciousness'	acknowledgement that her actions were unpredictable, inexplicable, thoughtless, …

continued ➤

Other features:

10   comment could be made on the sentence structure/tone of the final sentence – e.g. the questioning/dismissive tone shows her attitude of contempt towards her parents

11   the positioning of 'Now' at the start of the paragraph indicates the re-evaluation that is to come

12   the generally self-mocking tone in the second sentence – exaggeration and use of colloquialism such as 'daft', 'lunatic', ...

9   Read lines 52–65.

(a) **What does the expression 'social liberalisation' (line 57) mean?**   **2 U**

For full marks, both words should be successfully glossed, e.g. a relaxation, softening, less strict, ... attitude (1); to matters concerning lifestyle, sexual behaviour, ... (1).

Effective use of a word like 'permissiveness' will probably score 2 marks.

(b) **Explain in your own words as far as possible what critics of 'social liberalisation' believe is wrong with it.**   **2 U**

There must be some attempt to use own words. Blatant lifts: 0.

For full marks, answers should cover both of the following:

1   gloss on 'weaken social cohesion', e.g. cause society to be less unified, lead to a measure of breakdown in society, loosen the bonds between people/families

2   gloss on 'marginalise the family', e.g. cause the family to be seen as less important

(c) **What does the writer believe may be the truth about it?**   **1 U**

There must be some attempt to use own words. Blatant lifts: 0.

Gloss on '(merely a scary and difficult) period of adjustment', e.g. a time of change, transition, of coming to terms with new ideas, ...

10   To what extent do you find the ideas and language of the final paragraph (lines 66–72) appropriate as a conclusion to the passage as a whole?   **4 E**

For full marks an answer must address ideas and language in the final paragraph as well as demonstrate some awareness of the thrust of the passage as a whole. The appropriateness as a conclusion may well be implicit.

Marks will depend on the quality of comment. Reference alone: 0.

Possible answers:

Ideas:

1   starts with dramatic description of negative effects of the generation gap and moves to a more optimistic vision of the generations coming together, hence mirroring the main idea in the passage that things are getting better

continued ➤

> ## The Generation Gap

2   reference to 'lifelong parenting' returns to the argument in opening paragraphs, hence showing a rounding off of the argument

Language – reference could be made to any of the following:

3   (melo)dramatic words such as 'vast', 'clash', 'profound', 'chasm' … to reinforce the idea of the impact of the generation gap in the past

4   the use of 'Yet …' to introduce a possible concession, improvement

5   'set down the cudgels' – graphic image of peace

6   'sheer good sense' – simplicity of words/ideas

7   'commitment' – positive sense of involvement by both sides

8   'any old person' – deliberate colloquialism to end on friendly, relaxed note

9   optimistic tone generated by words/expressions such as 'settles down', 'good sense', 'commitment', 'help'

Question on both Passages

11   **Both writers approve of the change in attitudes revealed by the survey. Which one more successfully engaged your interest in her point of view?**

Justify your choice by referring closely to the style of writing of both passages.   **5 A/E**

Note that candidates are instructed to focus on style. Reference to the ideas of the passages is, of course, unavoidable and will in many cases strengthen the candidate's response.

The mark for this question should reflect the overall quality of the response and may not be directly related to the length of the response or to the number of points/references made. A succinct, sophisticated response should be worth more than a series of fairly trivial points and obvious references. 'Ticking and adding up' is not appropriate (or fair) here.

For full marks there must be reference to both passages (although not necessarily a balanced treatment) and convincing evaluative comment. Where reference is made to one passage only, the maximum mark is 3.

The following guidelines should be used:

5 marks   clear and intelligent understanding of style in both passages; effective references; evaluative comment is convincing

4 marks   clear understanding of style in both passages; sensible references; evaluative comment is reasonably convincing

continued ➤

The Generation Gap

3 marks understanding of style in both passages; adequate references; discernible evaluative comment

2 marks some understanding of style; limited reference; at least one appropriate evaluative comment

1 mark one or two relevant but unconvincing comments

The following points could be made, but all points which candidates propose will have to be judged on their merits:

Passage One:

light-hearted introduction	'enough motor function', 'weirdness dust'
tone of surprise at survey findings	'even chic'
occasional colloquialism	'cool', 'mum and dad'
some rather grand/grandiose imagery	'bedrock', 'social cohesion'
positive tone of conclusion	'it is merely changing', 'energy and courage is wonderful'

Passage Two:

fairly serious introduction	'long-term commitment', 'predicated upon', …
use of personal recollection	lines 38–51
self-awareness within the recollection	'daft', 'idiotic', 'lunatic' …
quite aggressive, violent imagery	'toxic trench', 'clashes', 'battles'
use of statistics (other than from survey)	'2% … 75%'
conclusion mostly positive	'settles down', 'commitment', 'recognise the obvious fact' – but some caution in 'maybe'

> **Paper Four**
>
> # Watch Your Words
>
> **Passage One:** Taking Politicians at their Words
>
> **Passage Two:** Weasel Words and Forked Tongues

Questions on Passage One

1   **Read lines 1–14.**

(a) **In your own words give two factors which 'Newspeak' in the novel *Nineteen Eighty-Four* and 'political language' as defined by Orwell in his 1946 essay seem to have in common.   2 U**

There must be some attempt to use own words. Blatant lifts: 0.

gloss on 'euphemism' (1)

gloss on 'circumlocution/cloudy vagueness/question begging' (1)

(b) **By referring to particular words or phrases, show how the example in lines 9–12 ('Defenceless ... pacification') illustrates one of these factors.   2 A**

'pacification' is a euphemism (1)

used to soften violent acts such as 'defenceless villages are bombarded from the air'/or any other of the statements (1)

(A case might be made for 'cloudy vagueness' and should be given some credit.)

2   **Read lines 15–23.**

(a) **Show how the word choice in lines 15–18 reveals the concerns of 'keen political watchers'.   2 A**

Marks will depend on the quality of comment. Reference alone: 0. An insightful comment on one example could gain more than 1 mark; a more basic comment will be worth 1 mark.

Any of the following examples with a comment suggesting that Unspeak is detrimental in some way:

1	'virulent'	rampant like a disease
2	'duplicitous'	double dealing/hidden/shameful
3	'stealth' in contrast with Newspeak	hiding intent/creeping/insinuating
4	'clumsy'	obvious/blundering/unintelligent

Watch Your Words

(b) **Show in detail how the comparison in lines 19–21 suggests that the writer regards Steven Poole as an effective campaigner against the political misuse of language?**　　2 A

Reference alone: 0. An explanation of the effectiveness of any two pairs of the points of the comparisons made here could be worth up to 2.

Steven Poole	rhetorical doublespeak
small boy	naked emperor
pin (to prick)	speech bubbles

3　**What does the sentence 'It is commonly thought…' (lines 29–31) tell us about politicians' language?**　　2 U

There must be some attempt to use own words. Blatant lifts: 0.

The candidate could refer to any two of the following:

1　politicians are thought to blether, talk emptily/profusely (1)

2　they attempt to pull the wool over our eyes (1)

3　but they actually reveal what their real intentions are (if the listener is alert) (1)

4　**Read lines 32–44.**

(a) **Explain fully why the term 'global warming' was changed to 'climate change' and what effect this change had.**　　3 U

There must be some attempt to use own words. Blatant lifts: 0.

Reasons for change:

1　countries with an interest in not making moves to stop global warming (because they made money from selling oil) (1)

and

2　tried to make it sound less threatening by having it officially called 'climate change' which sounded more neutral (1)

Effect of change:

3　as a result, action which should have been taken to prevent such rises has been delayed (1)

or

4　the countries and oilmen with a vested interest have benefited (1)

> *Watch Your Words*

(b) **Show how imagery and sentence structure in these lines assist in emphasising the writer's argument.** **4 A**

Marks will depend on the quality of comment. Reference alone: 0. An insightful comment on one example could gain up to 3 marks; a more basic comment will be worth 1 mark. Both sentence structure and imagery have to be dealt with to gain full marks.

Answers on imagery must 'deconstruct' the image, i.e. show an understanding of the literal root of the image and then explore how the writer is extending it figuratively.

Imagery:

1	'cog in the machinery'	as a cog is an important (but usually unseen) aid in the running of a machine so the words used in Unspeak have the effect of making the processes by which government works smooth and hidden and successful
2	'Carefully tooled phrases'	the words have been carefully chosen and developed to fit their purpose in the same way that parts of machinery have to be crafted carefully to an exact size and purpose to make sure that the machinery runs smoothly
3	'entrenched (political) position'	suggests that the policies and ideas of the government have been fixed and stuck in the same way that a military trench is dug to make a defensive position which cannot be easily attacked or overrun
4	'scattered like seed…'	examples of Unspeak are expressed abundantly and spread wide in order to create belief in the concepts in the same way that seed is widely scattered so that some at least will germinate

Points 1 and 2 could be dealt with together as an extended metaphor.

Sentence structure:

5	'The reason?'	short, abrupt question causes a sense of urgency to know what the answer might be
6	use of semi-colon before 'can refer…'	the semi colon followed by the 'can' without a pronoun continues the abrupt, matter of fact style suggesting that it is stating the obvious
7	'And it works:'	simple short, punchy statement – the 'And' at the beginning of the sentence stresses the inevitability of the result

continued ➢

| 8 | use of colon after 'works' | prepares the reader for an explanation of how Unspeak works and its results |

5 Show how the writer's word choice or imagery in lines 45–49 dramatises the 'abortion debate'.   **2 A**

Marks will depend on the quality of comment. Reference alone: 0. An insightful comment on one example could gain more than 1 mark; a more basic comment will be worth 1 mark.

There may be overlap between word choice and imagery. Be sympathetic to answers which do not seem to make a clear distinction. The 'dramatic' dimension may be implicit in the analysis.

Word choice/imagery:

1	'lock horns'	literally suggests that the two sides are engaged in furious conflict like stags/goats clashing together and getting entangled in the same way that the debate is fierce and is never concluded – they are stuck
2	'rallying'	suggests the idea of demonstrating publicly to back up their views as troops massing to defend their position
3	'label'	suggests that they were all classified/recognisable under the same brand name – were easily (and proudly) identifiable
4	'gazumped'	suggests the idea of going one better, topping their attempt with something more effective (like a housebuyer offering more to secure a deal over someone who thought he already had it)
5	'plumped'	suggests a lucky or effective choice, something they went for quickly

Comment on any of the terms 'pro-choice', 'pro-life' and 'anti-life' in isolation would be unlikely to give rise to any developed comment. A comment which relates them by degree or contrast could be worth one mark.

6 'All Unspeak terms have a shelf life.' (line 50)

In your own words explain how this idea is developed in lines 50–61.   **2 U**

There must be some attempt to use own words. Blatant lifts: 0.

The idea that there is a limited period of time during which an example of Unspeak is effective is shown by:

| 1 | 'concentration camp' which was used for internment camps and became impossible to use when it became associated with the Holocaust (2) |

continued ➤

> *Watch Your Words*

2 'climate change' which seemed acceptable and delayed progress until people woke up to what it really meant (2)

An answer which claims that the idea is developed by the use of examples (unspecified) may be worth 1 mark.

7   Read lines 62–70.

These two paragraphs contain advice from the writer and from Orwell on what we can do to combat the deceptive uses of language. Which of these paragraphs seems to you to give more vivid expression to the advice? Justify your choice by referring to the language of both paragraphs.   **4 A/E**

There are no marks available for a simple statement of preference. Marks will depend on the quality of evaluative comment relating to 'vivid' but preference may be implicit in the answer. Reference alone: 0. An insightful comment on one example could gain more than 1 mark; a more basic comment will be worth 1 mark.

Reference might be made to any of the following features in any combination:

Word choice/imagery:

Didcock – lines 62–65:

1	'look behind'	suggests investigating/calling bluff
2	'hiding in the murk'	suggests something unpleasant lurking in the darkness/recesses

Orwell – lines 66–70:

3	'jeers'	suggests attacking by scorn or contempt
4	'worn out'	suggests beyond its shelf life/no longer functioning
5	'useless'	suggests beneath contempt
6	'dustbin'	suggests appropriate place for useless broken items (rubbish)
7	'belongs'	suggests contemptuous dismissal/obvious resting place

Sentence structure:

Didcock – lines 62–65:

8   practical question followed by a simple answer (in a nutshell)

9   three repeated commands 'complain' 'look' 'see' expand on the simple answer

Orwell – lines 66–70

10   advisory realistic comments – 'one cannot...'

continued ➤

11   complex sentence building to a climax 'dustbin, where it belongs.'

12   use of comma (line 70) to isolate the climax 'where it belongs'.

Tone:

Identification of tone must be related to reference (probably to some of the above points) and should be accompanied by an appropriate linking comment.

Didcock – lines 62–65:

13   direct, practical, confident, no nonsense…

Orwell – lines 66–70:

14   cautious, dismissive, advisory, scornful, reflective…

15   Other language features should be treated on their merits.

8   **Choose one of Didcock's own examples from lines 74–75 and explain why you think it appropriate for inclusion as 'Unspeak'.**   **2 U**

Marks will depend on the quality of comment. Reference alone: 0. Credit up to 2 marks can be given for one example. No marks for a second example.

1	'collateral damage'	death or destruction that happens to someone outside the target area – seemingly implying no fault of the perpetrator; in fact disguises carelessness or incompetence
2	'smart bomb'	missile that seems almost positively intelligent/commendable but still destroys/results in death/and may be off target
3	'surgical strike'	the use of force on a target that disguises it in a suggestion of exactitude and cleanliness – but which actually causes messy deaths

9   **Explain why the writer saves 'repetitive administration of legitimate force' as the example for the final paragraph. (lines 76–77)**   **1 A**

Any of the following answers for 1 mark.

1   sums up what he has been dealing with in the passage in a very shocking way, with a really violent example

2   example injects a bit of humour/irony suggests that this is what should happen to the politicians

3   its meaning is appropriate to the end of the passage because it suggests finality in 'beating to death'

Watch Your Words

Questions on Passage Two

10 Read lines 1–8.

   (a) **Identify the two differing attitudes to a 'war on terror', one on the part of the military and one on the part of the politicians.**   **2 U**

Blatant lifts: 0.

The military regard it as impossible/stupid/unwinnable/absurd. (1)

The politicians regard it with favour/find it appealing/useful tactic. (1)

   (b) **Show how word choice or sentence structure in these lines reveals each of these attitudes.**   **2 A**

Marks will depend on the quality of comment. Reference alone: 0. An insightful comment on one example could gain more than 1 mark; a more basic comment will be worth 1 mark.

Word choice/imagery:

Military:

1	'factor in'/'surrender'/'treaties'/'battle'	these aspects of a war – strategic planning, careful preparation, practical end result – are inapplicable in face of the 'war on terror'
2	'threat from abstract nouns'	danger cannot be dealt with or planned for in military terms

Politicians:

3	'smuggle'	underhand, secretive, illegal activity allows them to hide their intentions
4	'extreme measures –'	suggest that politicians can hide nasty processes under the pretext
5	'detention'/'torture...'	repressive dictatorial actions justified in peacetime if you call it 'war'

Sentence structure:

Military:

6	series of short sentences (lines 4–5)	suggests military precision/dismissal
7	repetition of 'cannot'	reinforces their denial that there is a real enemy/that war on terror is possible

continued ➤

Politicians:

8	parenthesis (line 7)	details the actual brutality of the extreme measures which the politicians are deviously pursuing under the guise of a non-existent 'war'
9	three examples (line 7) 'detention ... abroad'	build up to a climax of normally unacceptable government behaviour showing how much they can get off with

11 Read lines 9–22.

(a) **What is ironic about describing teenagers as 'anti-social'? (line 12)**   2 U

There must be some attempt to use own words. Blatant lifts: 0.

Teenagers in groups are seen as disruptive/threatening/furtively dressed when actually all they are doing is behaving in a normally social gregarious way.

(b) **Explain fully why the writer is disturbed by the concept of ASBOs.**   2 A

There must be some attempt to use own words. Blatant lifts: 0.

Each of the following explanations would be worth 2 marks. A more basic answer might be worth 1 mark.

actions which are merely discomfiting to other members of society can be classed as criminal under an ASBO (2)

an ASBO allows the state to intrude into private life with heavy handed punishment more typical of dictatorships (than our supposed democracy) (2)

12 Read lines 23–27.

Show how imagery in these lines is effective in condemning the misuse of language by politicians.   2 A

Answers on imagery must 'deconstruct' the image, i.e. show an understanding of the literal root of the image and then explore how the writer is extending it figuratively.

1	'ooze'	suggests unpleasant pus/thick sludge emerging from an infected wound/depths of the earth, applied to anti-democratic habit suggests unpleasant/rotten/insidious
2	'breaks the crust'	suggests the unsightly scab/scum over the lava which covers the unpleasantness/danger underneath
3	'spin doctors'	suggests experts in curing/patching up who use their skill to present failures in a positive light/airbrush disasters in the same way that a bowler puts spin on a ball to deceive a batsman

continued ➤

Watch Your Words

| 4 | 'cousin' | suggests Unspeak belongs to the same family of deception as Newspeak/is closely related/shares the same values |

13 Read lines 28–33.

(a) In your own words explain what is meant by 'pushing a partisan agenda'.   1 U

There must be some attempt to use own words. Blatant lifts: 0.

Journalists can be lazy and just use the terms that politicians want them to without bothering to see what lies behind them

(b) How do the origin and development of the phrase 'ethnic cleansing' illustrate the danger of politically promoted terms?   2 U

Any two of the following for 1 mark each:

1 'ethnic cleansing' was a euphemistic term applied to a process of maintaining purity by mass murder

2 attention was drawn to its euphemistic quality by always putting it into inverted commas to show that it was the reverse of admirable

3 if the inverted commas are omitted it suggests that we have become so used to the phrase that it seems acceptable

14 'Purge' was used by Stalin as a euphemism for what was, in fact, a massacre.

What is any one of the other euphemisms in lines 39–41 designed to disguise?   1 U

Any of the following for 1 mark:

1	'management shake-up'	demoting some people
2	'corporate downshift'	slashing size/sacking people
3	'cabinet reshuffle'	getting rid of some ministers

15 (a) Show how sentence structure in lines 42–47 gives impact to Behr's analysis of Steven Poole's views.   2 A

Marks will depend on the quality of comment. Reference alone: 0. An insightful comment on one example could gain more than 1 mark; a more basic comment will be worth 1 mark.

| 1 | 'but' (line 42) | Behr balances admiration for Poole's analysis against criticism of its bleakness |
| 2 | 'Not every metaphor…' (line 43) | the short authoritative pronouncement makes the criticism stronger |

continued ➤

<table>
<tr>
<td>3</td>
<td>'But...more likely...' (line 45)</td>
<td>beginning the sentence unusually with 'But' throws stronger weight on the criticism (of Poole's over-eagerness to see deviousness)</td>
</tr>
<tr>
<td>4</td>
<td>'No less...but...' (line 47)</td>
<td>the balanced brief final non-sentence shows sympathy with Poole but decisively rejects his view/sums up neatly his scepticism of Poole's claims</td>
</tr>
</table>

(b) **Do you agree or disagree that the last sentence (lines 49–50) is an effective end to the passage? Briefly justify your answer.** **1 E**

For: ends on an optimistic note in line with the previous paragraph/showing the same balanced structure (1)

or

Against: there is nothing anywhere leading up to this optimism (1)

Question on both Passages

16 Which writer is more successful in convincing you that the problem of Unspeak is a serious matter. Justify your choice by referring to the ideas of both passages. **5 U/E**

Note that the question asks for concentration on ideas alone.

The mark for this question should reflect the overall quality of the response and may not be directly related to the length of the response or to the number of points/references made. A succinct, sophisticated response should be worth more than a series of fairly trivial points and obvious references. 'Ticking and adding up' is not appropriate (or fair) here.

For full marks there must be reference to both passages (although not necessarily a balanced treatment) and convincing evaluative comment. Where reference is made to one passage only, the maximum mark is 3.

The following guidelines should be used:

5 marks   clear and intelligent understanding of ideas in both passages; effective references; evaluative comment is convincing

4 marks   clear understanding of ideas in both passages; sensible references; evaluative comment is reasonably convincing

3 marks   understanding of ideas in both passages; adequate references; discernible evaluative comment

2 marks   some understanding of ideas; limited reference; at least one appropriate evaluative comment

1 mark   one or two relevant but unconvincing comments.

continued ➢

> *Watch Your Words*

Passage One:

Those finding Passage One more successful might cite some of the following ideas:

the use of language as a weapon

the argument explores the problem and provides a practical solution

use of both Orwell's and Poole's ideas

uses more examples to show the strengths and duplicity of: war on terror/climate change/abortion debate

optimistically shows the temporary nature of the power of these words

provides solutions to the problem: be aware of language misuse and stop using terms thoughtlessly

Passage Two:

Those finding Passage Two more successful might cite some of the following ideas:

contrasts the military with politician's attitude to the use of language as weapon

Behr shows concern about democracy and the misuse of power

Behr feels that politicians use vague language to allow them to cover up dictatorial tendencies (detention without trial, torture…)

in domestic terms this process allows governments to interfere too far in what should be private life by criminalising fairly normal behaviour

this interference is typical of dictatorships rather than democracies

by controlling words and distorting them the truth is manipulated (ethnic cleansing, extraordinary rendition, purge, tragedy…)

perhaps Poole's criticisms pushed too far, too suspiciously

although Behr demonstrates the continuing power of the phrases to conceal the truth, he feels that not all of Poole's examples are as duplicitous as Poole makes out

(over) optimistic conclusion that truth will win

Paper Five

Christmas

Passage One: Blame the Victorians

Passage Two: 'What Are You Doing for Christmas?'

Questions on Passage One

1   **Read lines 1–11.**

    (a) **Why, according to the writer in these lines, is Christmas particularly hard for women? 2 U**

There must be some attempt to use own words. Blatant lifts: 0.

Any two of the following for 1 mark each:

1   the task of deciding on presents falls to them

2   the task of acquiring the presents falls to them

3   they are put under great stress/have to work very hard

4   they have to live up to a stereotype

5   they don't get sufficient recognition for their efforts

    (b) **Referring to more than one example, show how the writer creates a light-hearted tone in these lines.   2 A**

Marks will depend on quality of comment. For full marks there must be reference to more than one example, although the same feature (e.g. exaggeration) could be dealt with by reference to more than one example. Reference alone: 0.

Possible answers:

1	'manic look'	exaggeration
2	'We're hardly capable …'	ironic, self-mocking use of first person
3	'frantic'	exaggeration
4	'mulled wine and mince pies'	gentle, homely, trivial details to contrast with (allegedly) deranged actions
5	'peer into our brains'	cartoon-like idea
6	'power station's worth'	hyperbole

continued ➤

> *Christmas*

| 7 | ' – and actually finding it' | added point after pause to emphasise humorously that it's even worse than it seems |
| 8 | 'a mysterious, elusive man' | humorous allusion to Santa Claus |

2   Read lines 12–26.

(a) **Show how the writer's word choice in lines 12–19 makes clear her view of the 'Victorian Christmas'.**   **2 A**

Marks will depend on the quality of comment. Insightful comment on one word could score 2 marks; more basic comments will be worth 1 mark. Reference alone: 0.

Possible answers:

1	'blame'	suggests culpability, feelings of resentment, bitterness, …
2	'invented'	suggests made up, hint of falseness
3	'ingeniously'	suggests element of craftiness, deceit
4	'turning'	suggests twisting, distorting true nature
5	'sober'/'religious'	suggests what they destroyed was noble, serious, valuable, …
6	'great festival'	suggests overblown, exaggerated event
7	'months'	exaggerates to suggest how extensive the preparations have to be
8	'got worse'	implication that it was bad enough, now even more demanding
9	'fiddling'	suggests trivial, purposeless action required to live up to the ideal

(b) **Show how the writer's sentence structure in lines 12–19 helps to clarify her view.   2 A**

Marks will depend on the quality of comment. Insightful comment on one feature could score 2 marks; more basic comments will be worth 1 mark. Mere identification of feature: 0.

Possible answers:

| 1 | first sentence | short, blunt, suggests it's a simple, undisputed fact |
| 2 | parenthetical list ('trees … togetherness') | to show extent of things Victorians 'invented' |

continued ➤

Christmas

3 colon   to introduce 'proof' that it 'had got worse'

4 'not only … but …'   highlights idea of increasing demand

(c) Explain in your own words two factors which, according to lines 20–26, make it more difficult to cope with Christmas now than in Victorian times.   2 U

There must be some attempt to use own words. Blatant lifts: 0.

The following two points should be made for 1 mark each:

1 the absence of domestic help, servants (idea of 'a lot of help' alone is not enough)

2 modern acquisitiveness, increase in expectations for gifts, commercial pressures

3 Read lines 27–52.

(a) Explain in your own words what it is that the writer finds 'intriguing'. (line 27) 1 U

There must be some attempt to use own words. Blatant lifts: 0.

An acceptable gloss on '(struggle to deliver) an essentially 19th-century festival', e.g. we haven't brought it up to date, we try to do it as it was done over 100 years ago, …

(The focus should be on the lack of change rather than on the 'struggle'.)

(b) Explain in your own words why, according to the writer in lines 31–42, the Victorians made 'such a big deal of Christmas'.   2 U

There must be some attempt to use own words. Blatant lifts: 0.

Marks will depend on the quality of explanation. For full marks an answer should touch on both of the following points:

1 the growth of industry/factories had fragmented/disrupted family life

2 Christmas was a way of rebuilding/restoring the importance/centrality of family life

(c) Why, according to the writer in lines 43–52, is there a desire nowadays for 'the perfect children's Christmas'? (line 47)   2 U

There must be some attempt to use own words. Blatant lifts: 0.

Any of the following for up to 2 marks, depending on the quality of explanation:

1 more time away from children because of increased work has led to a desire to compensate by making Christmas something really special

2 a recognition that children's lives are more stressful creates a desire to compensate by making Christmas something really special

3 in a dangerous/threatening world, we are deeply conscious of the need to preserve childhood as something special

Christmas

4 **How effective do you find the writer's comparison of the way we behave at Christmas to 'emotional bulimia'? (line 53)** **3 A/E**

Marks will depend on the quality of comment. For full marks an answer should show a clear understanding of the way the writer links the 'binge' idea contained in 'bulimia' with the way we cram so much into celebrating Christmas, and contain some appropriate evaluative comment, e.g. that she is being very critical, since bulimia is an illness.

5 **Read lines 58–70.**

(a) **Why is the Victorian Christmas 'close to breaking point'? (line 58)** **1 U**

There must be some attempt to use own words. Blatant lifts: 0.

Women nowadays do not have the time.

(b) **What does the writer see as an advantage of 'the escape fantasy'? (line 61)** **1 U**

There must be some attempt to use own words. Blatant lifts: 0.

Either of the following for 1 mark:

1   it will make things easier for women

2   it will reduce stress within families

(c) **What disadvantages does she see in it?** **2 U**

There must be some attempt to use own words. Blatant lifts: 0.

Both of the following for 1 mark each:

1   it will be less private, less family-orientated

2   it will depend on low-paid staff to provide the service/it will perpetuate the need for cheap labour (in the destination countries)

6 **Read lines 71–78.**

(a) **Why, according to the writer, will globalisation 'modernise Christmas'?** **2 U**

There must be some attempt to use own words. Blatant lifts: 0.

For full marks there should be at least an implicit understanding of what is meant by 'globalisation' plus an appropriate reference to at least one of the following:

1   the impact of technology, of the '24/7' economy, will make the current model impossible

2   we will no longer be able to go our own way

3   work patterns are already having an impact

(b) **How effective do you find the last sentence of this paragraph as a conclusion to the passage as a whole?** **3 E**

Answers could refer to the style or ideas or both. For full marks there must be a clear focus on the sentence and sensible reference to the thrust of the passage as a whole.

Possible points:

1   it reasserts the notion that our current approach to Christmas is outdated

2   the rhetorical question, which invites a very clear answer

3   it returns to the original focus on women's role

4   'relied on' emphasises the dependence on women

5   'show' reinforces the idea of Christmas as a production, something created for effect

6   the flippant tone of 'keep the show going'

Questions on Passage Two

7   **Read lines 1–12.**

(a) **By referring to any two examples, show how the writer's punctuation in these lines helps to clarify his argument.** **2 A**

Answers must be specific about what the writer is actually saying in these paragraphs. No marks for merely identifying the punctuation marks.

Any two of the following for 1 mark each:

1   colon introduces expansion of opening statement about 'the vast majority of new books …'

2   brackets include additional evidence about sales in November/December

3   semicolon separates two pieces of evidence about sales

4   dashes include expansion/explanation of 'the great TV beasts'

5   commas in the parenthetical list separate the items

(b) **Why does the writer think that for 'serious' writers Christmas is a 'disastrous time in which to have a new book published'? (line 7)** **1 U**

There must be some attempt to use own words. Blatant lifts: 0.

Sales are dominated by high-volume, 'popular', light-weight, easy reading, …

Christmas

(c) **Explain fully how the extended imagery in lines 8–12 makes clear the writer's point.**   **4 A**

Marks will depend on the quality of comment. Mere identification of words in the extended image: 0. For full marks there should be sensible and relevant comment on at least three of the words/expressions listed below, especially points 1 and 2. Evaluation may be implicit.

Answers on imagery should 'de-construct' the image, i.e. show a clear acknowledgement of the literal root and of how the writer is extending this figuratively.

Possible references and comment:

1	'tender shoots'	compares quality writing to vulnerable young plants in early stages of growth, suggestion of requiring careful nurturing, protection
2	'crushed underfoot'	compares fate of quality writing to destruction by marauding beasts
3	'bellowing herd'	compares popular works to large, aggressive, destructive animals
4	'(publishing) jungle'	compares world of publishing to unregulated, dangerous environment
5	'stampede'	compares popular works (and/or their purchasers) to violent, destructive force, lacking independent thought

8   *(a)* **Why does the writer find the trend he has described in paragraphs 1 and 2 'culturally depressing'? (line 13)**   **1 U**

There must be some attempt to use own words. Blatant lifts: 0.

Any of the following for 1 mark:

1   the reliance on unchallenging books/sidelining of more serious work

2   seeing books as commodities/reliance on appearance

3   the fact that many books given as gifts will not be read

(b) **Show how the writer creates a dismissive tone in lines 13–18.**   **2 A**

Marks will depend on the quality of comment. Insightful comment on one word or expression could earn 2 marks; more basic comments will be worth 1 mark. Reference alone: 0.

Possible answers:

1	'shifting'	implies thoughtless attitude of publishers, books as objects, commodities, …
2	'objects'	as above

continued ➤

3	'nice'	deliberately ineffective word to suggest the shallowness of vendors/purchasers
4	'find their way'	as if the books do it themselves, recipients show no interest
5	'seat beside the loo'	lavatorial reference to emphasise how little pride recipients take in the gift
6	'(no more than a) polite glance'	highlights superficiality of response – brief, uninterested, despite appearance of respect

9   Read lines 19–35.

(a) **Explain in your own words the 'wider sickness' to which the writer refers in lines 19–28.** **2 U**

There must be some attempt to use own words. Blatant lifts: 0.

Any of the following for 1 mark each:

1   we place too much emphasis on Christmas

2   we expect Christmas to compensate for lack of attention to friends, etc. during the rest of the year

3   we do not even look forward to Christmas any more

4   Christmas has become loveless, something of a chore, …

(b) **Show how the writer's imagery in lines 29–35 illustrates his dissatisfaction with Christmas.** **4 A**

Marks will depend on the quality of comment. Insightful comment on one image could earn 2 or even, exceptionally, 3 marks; more basic comments will be worth 1 mark. Mere identification of image: 0.

Answers on imagery should 'de-construct' the image, i.e. show a clear acknowledgement of the literal root and of how the writer is extending this figuratively.

Possible answers:

1	'shoe-horns'	just as a shoe-horn forces, squeezes the foot into the shoe, so Christmas is used as a way of compressing a year's attentions into a few days
2	'showered'	compares the lavishing of presents on children to drenching from rainfall
3	'drying up … irrigated'	comparing relationships to plants, crops reduces their significance, …

continued ➢

Christmas

| 4 | 'irrigated with booze' | contemptuous comparison of alcohol with provision of water necessary for growth |

10 **Read lines 36–46.**

   (a) **Explain briefly in your own words the writer's solution to the problem.**   **1 U**

There must be some attempt to use own words. Blatant lifts: 0.

We should stop concentrating our social lives on such a short period of time/should try to be sociable all year round.

   (b) **In what way is January a 'boom-time … for our learned friends, the lawyers'?**   **1 U**

There must be some attempt to use own words. Blatant lifts: 0.

They get a lot of business, money (because of fall-outs, disputes which occur at Christmas).

Question on both Passages

11 **Which passage, in your opinion, gives a more convincing description of the problems and difficulties caused by Christmas?**

Justify your choice by detailed reference to the ideas of both passages.   **5 U/E**

Note that the question asks for concentration on ideas alone.

The mark for this question should reflect the overall quality of the response and may not be directly related to the length of the response or to the number of points/references made. A succinct, sophisticated response should be worth more than a series of fairly trivial and obvious references. 'Ticking and adding up' is not appropriate (or fair) here.

For full marks there must be reference to both passages (although not necessarily a balanced treatment) and convincing evaluative comment. Where reference is made to one passage only, the maximum mark is 3.

The following guidelines should be followed:

5 marks   intelligent understanding of both passages; ability to compare/contrast ideas is strong

4 marks   clear understanding of both passages; ability to compare/contrast ideas is evident

3 marks   understanding of both passages; some ability to compare/contrast ideas is discernible

2 marks   some understanding of both passages; limited ability to compare/contrast ideas

1 mark   one or two relevant but unconvincing points

continued ➤

Christmas

The following points could be made, but all points which candidates propose will have to be judged on their merits:

Passage One:

starts with focus on problems posed for women at Christmas

gives historical background, explains differences between now and Victorian times

explains reasons for Victorians' elevation of Christmas

describes impact of industrialisation, capitalism

the 'emotional bulimia' point

looks at possible future developments, the 'escape fantasy'

considers the impact of globalisation

Passage Two:

starts with focus on publishing/bookselling/problems for writers

explores 'wider sickness' of the way Christmas has become distorted

Christmas as a time of 'stress and loneliness'

suggests need to avoid concentrating so much into a short period

recognises that it's good for at least one group

Paper Six

Mountains of the Mind

Passage One: Mountains of the Mind

Passage Two: Summit Fever

Questions on Passage One

1   **Read lines 1–11.**

   (a) **What kind of landscape appealed to the seventeenth century imagination?**   **1 U**

There must be some attempt to use own words. Blatant lifts: 0.

Answers should show an understanding of:

domesticated/managed for food production/orderly and neat

   (b) **By referring to two examples from these lines, show how word choice used to describe this landscape demonstrates its appeal to the people of the time.**   **2 A**

Marks will depend on the quality of comment on the connotations of the words. Reference alone: 0. Two examples must be dealt with for full marks.

1	'(agricultural) fecundity'	feeling of fertile growth, plenty
2	'rich (ridges)'	productive, generous
3	'crop lands'	producing foodstuff, managed
4	'ideal (components)'	highly appropriate, proper, perfect
5	'tamed'	impression of control, rendered safe
6	'(human) order'	man was in control
7	'the plough, the hedgerow, the ditch'	these kept things in line, controlled

2   **Referring to lines 12–16 ('… rigid'), show how the two dangers associated with mountains are highlighted by the imagery the writer uses to describe each.**   **4 A**

Marks will depend on the quality of comment. Reference alone: 0. An insightful comment on one example could earn more than 1 mark; a more basic comment will be worth 1 mark.

Answers on imagery must 'deconstruct' the image, i.e. show an understanding of the literal root of the image and then explore how the writer is extending it figuratively.

continued ➤

Mountains of the Mind

Avalanches:

1	'triggered'/'loaded'	small movement producing large effects in the same way that the lightest touch on the trigger of a loaded gun causes it to go off
2	'light as a cough'	the comparison to a cough shows how tiny is the volume of sound which acts as a stimulus in such a vast arena
3	'foot of a beetle'	comparison to something so minute in size as a beetle's foot causing such dangerous effects is alarming
4	'brush of a bird's wing'	the comparison between something so silent, and so fragile as the 'brush' of such a small thing as a bird's wing shows how easily danger is created

Crevasses:

5	'blue jaws'	the image of a shark's jaws opening to catch its prey is being compared to the effect of the ice waiting like an open slit ready to clamp and trap the climber emphasising the danger of the crevasse
6	'regurgitated'	continues the image of being 'eaten' by the crevasse as by a shark before being vomited out some time later, as a trapped body eventually would reach the surface in a mangled state
7	'pulped'	continues the image by suggesting the effects of mastication or digestion on a shark's prey are like those created by the grinding of the ice in a glacier
8	'rigid'	frozen stiff suggesting the corpse would be completely immovable as a steel bar

3 **Show how the sentence 'During the second half ... splendour of a mountainous landscape' (lines 22–24) acts as a link in the writer's line of thought. You should refer to specific words or phrases from the sentence in your answer.** **2 U**

'travel to mountains out of a spirit other than necessity' refers back to the idea of travelling in mountains only when unavoidable. (1)

'of the splendour of a mountainous landscape' refers forward to the beauty of the mountains referred to later on in the paragraph. (1)

continued ➤

> Mountains of the Mind

'However' – a comment making an acceptable point about its linking function – probably to do with time – could be worth up to 1.

Answers which try to make a time link with reference to 'second half of the 1700s' can probably make a case only for the link forward – possibly worth 1 mark.

4 **(a)** **Read lines 34–40 ('. . . wilderness').**

Explain in your own words why the attraction of mountains is important to 'urbanised Western culture'. **2 U**

There must be some attempt to use own words. Blatant lifts: 0.

Any of the following for up to 2 marks, depending on the quality of explanation.

1   city dwellers are desperate for some space and wilderness after being enclosed in cities for too long

2   city dwellers feel a need for the spiritual experience which they feel comes from experience of the wild and beautiful because they feel smothered in the mundane aspects of city life

3   contrast between the materialistic life of cities and the spiritual world of the mountains

(b) **What two main pieces of evidence are presented in the remainder of this paragraph (lines 40–45) to prove the popularity of mountain going? Use your own words as far as possible in your answer.** **2 U**

There must be some attempt to use own words. Blatant lifts: 0.

1   (Statistics show that) a large number of people go mountaineering/hillwalking (1)

2   (Statistics show that) a great deal of money is spent on equipment/support for this pursuit (1)

5 **Read lines 46–49.**

Show how this paragraph fulfils an important function in the structure of the passage up to this point. **2 A**

1 Any identification of a summing up aspect (1)

and any one of the following

2 that it covers the history of a revolution (1)

or

3 that it shows the progress from avoidance to acceptance of mountains (1)

or

4 an appropriate comment on 'therefore', e.g. signifying a deduction (1)

> Mountains of the Mind

6 *(a)* **Read lines 50–57.**

What is the meaning of the phrase 'culturally devised'. (line 52) 1 U

gloss on 'culturally devised' i.e. invented to conform to our own society's values/invented by society as part of our view about the world

(b) **How does the content of the remainder of the paragraph from 'That is to say…' (line 52) expand on this idea?** 2 U

An answer which glosses two of the following ideas is likely to be worth two marks:

1 'qualities' – we impose our own meanings on a landscape

2 'values' – we judge what we 'see' according to our own human priorities

3 'useless obstructions' – we used to see mountains only as a nuisance, an impediment to travel

4 'exquisite forms' – we see them now as high in the scale of beauty/in an artistic way

A simple gloss on 'we do not see…think is there' – e.g. 'We see things not as they are but as we want to see them' would be worth 1 mark.

7 *(a)* **Read lines 58–69.**

'Mountains are only contingencies of geology.' (lines 61–62)

In your own words explain the meaning of this sentence and show how the meaning is clarified by any one of the statements which follow it. 2 U

Reference or quotation alone: 0.

meaning of the sentence:

mountains are accidental formations of rock caused by random movements of the earth's surface (1)

and

clarification:

any one of the following for 1 mark:

1 'they do not kill deliberately….'   they have no will or mind to do so

2 'Mountains are simply there'   they have no feelings

3 'They exist over and …perceptions'   they sit there regardless of whether there are any human beings to enthuse about them or not

(b) **Show how sentence structure in these lines helps to clarify the explanation.** 2 A

Marks will depend on the quality of comment. Reference alone: 0. Mere identification of feature: 0. An insightful comment on one feature could score up to 2 marks; a more basic comment will be worth 1 mark.

continued ➤

Mountains of the Mind

1	'They do not kill…please' balanced clauses (actually chiasmus) pivoting on semi-colon	restatement and inversion increase the emphasis on the fact that they have no feelings
2	repetition of '(not)deliberately'/ '(nor) deliberately'	emphasises their neutrality
3	use of the colon in line 63	to introduce an expansion of the same unemotional ideas which occur before the colon, but in a more generalised way
4	the list or grouping of natural (extreme) environments in parenthesis (lines 64–65)	gives a series of examples of other environments which humans have romanticised, like mountains, equally stupidly/misguidedly
5	the isolation of 'are simply there'	makes simple blunt and effective statement in contrast with the complex list preceding it
6	repetition of 'there' (line 66)	emphasises that mountains are independent of us/do not have any properties except their physical and geological position
7	use of 'But' at beginning of last sentence	sums up the contradiction that, in fact, our imaginations have manufactured an emotional importance for mountains
8	use of semi-colon in line 69	it connects/balances two parts of the sentence, each of which repeats the same ideas about imagination

8   How does the language of the final paragraph (lines 70–79) bring out the contrast between the imagined and the real experience of mountains? You may wish to consider such features as sentence structure, word choice, imagery, sound…   **4 A**

Marks will depend on the quality of comment. Reference alone: 0. Mere identification of feature: 0. An insightful comment on one example/feature could score more than 2 marks; more basic comments on several features could add up to 4.

Word choice:

Comment on any of these words or phrases showing contrast could be worth up to 2 marks.

1	'hand's touch'	'mind's eye'
2	'mountains of the earth'	'mountains of the mind'
3	'hard'/'steep'/'sharp rock'/ 'freezing snow'	'gazes'/'reads'/'dreams'/'desires'
4	'of vertigo…frostbite'	'of unspeakable beauty'

continued ➤

Mountains of the Mind

Imagery:

Answers on imagery must 'deconstruct' the image, i.e. show an understanding of the literal root of the image and then explore how the writer is extending it figuratively.

5	'mind's eye'	as if the impressions were 'seen' in the mind rather than through the physical sense of sight, gives the impression of an active imagination contrasting with the physicality of 'the hand's touch'
6	'mountains of the mind'	the writer is making the contrast between the physical objects in a landscape and the idea that these mountains occupy our imaginations so much that they loom up in our thoughts, dominating our feelings

Sentence structure:

7	balance in sentence beginning 'Stone, rock...'	parallel structure strengthens the contrast between the appeal to the imagination and the hardness of the rock
8	list or climactic series of verbs in sentence beginning 'The mountain one gazes at...'	escalating nature of list followed by the last negative simple statement adds impact to the contrast
9	list or catalogue of all the drawbacks in the sentence beginning 'The latter are...'	impact of the number and type of physical discomforts contributes to an overwhelmingly harsh impression which contrasts with the beauty
10	the use of semi-colons in the sentence 'The latter are..'	calls attention to each of the items between the semi-colons and, by slowing down the sentence, allows each item to be given due weight/building up to a climax of physical discomfort to contrast with the brevity of the statement about the beauty
11	use of 'And' at beginning of last sentence (line 78)	unusual use of 'And' draws attention to the importance of the beauty in contrast with the negative nature of what has gone before
12	short last sentence (line 78)	spare simplicity of sentence emphasises the beauty in contrast with the packed nature of the hazards in the sentence before

Sound:

13   Comments on the cadence of the balanced structures or the dying fall of the last sentence should be marked on their merits.

continued ➤

> *Mountains of the Mind*

14 Other language features should be marked under the same principles as above. No mark for identification of feature. Marks available only for comment.

Questions on Passage Two

9 How effective is the simile in lines 1–2 in showing the writer's fascination with mountaineering?   **2 A/E**

An appropriate explanation such as the following could gain 2 marks.

The surprising comparison of monastic life (a serious commitment, not just a pastime) to mountaineering (normally seen as a hobby rather than a way of life) makes mountaineering seem a much more consuming passion, not just an ordinary (trivial) leisure activity.

A more basic answer which does not refer to the pastime/hobby aspect could be worth 1 mark.

10 *(a)* What does the description of 'Good Brit Style' in lines 5–11 reveal about his and his friends' attitude to mountaineering?   **2 U**

Blatant lifts: 0.
they pretended that they weren't serious about it/fooled around/didn't train seriously/didn't keep fit/weren't organised (1)

but, in fact, they did care and were (surprisingly) successful (1)

** *(b)* Show how the writer's sentence structure in these lines adds to the impact of his description of Good Brit Style.**   **2 A**

Marks will depend on the quality of comment. Reference alone: 0. Mere identification of feature: 0. An insightful comment on one feature could score up to 2 marks; a more basic comment will be worth 1 mark.

1	use of colon after 'elements of Good Brit Style:' (line 7)	raises the expectation that there will be an explanation of what these elements are; introduces a list of those elements which ironically seem not to be 'Good'
2	list of elements after the same colon (line 7)	series of prohibitions of activities (like training) which would normally be seen as desirable
3	climactic list in sentence 'To drink...	series of things to do which seem undesirable – like drinking too much – leading up to the positive contrast – the unexpected result – 'and still climb it'
4	climax in sentence 'To drink...'	lengthening of each element in the list till the climax (the unexpected result) is reached '*and still climb it*'
5	use of italics in line 10	enhances the climax and its monosyllabic brief nature makes it seem more triumphant

continued ➤

Mountains of the Mind

| 6 | clause after the colon in line 10 | sums up the preceding details of good style in an emphatic way |
| 7 | clause starting with 'that' (line 10) | creates a smug, triumphant, self-congratulatory tone by the emphasis on 'that' at the beginning of the clause . |

11 **'It was, quite simply, very exciting; it dramatised my life.' (line 20)**

Show how the sentence structure in lines 12–19 demonstrates the excitement or the drama of his experience. **2 A**

Marks will depend on the quality of explanation.

Sentence structure:

1	use of contrast/balanced clauses: 'promise and threat … enjoyed rather than suffered' 'Weekdays were a time for recovery and appreciation…weekends to both dread and anticipate.'	suggests that there are mixed reactions, a tension between two emotions which causes excitement/drama
2	series of items listed after 'My social life…'	gives the impression of busy experiences based round climbing – making life exciting
3	the minor sentence 'Much laughter, abuse…'	creates the impression of a lot of experiences packed into the same time, creating a turmoil of emotions leading to an exciting atmosphere

12 **By referring to lines 21–25, explain why he felt unprepared for climbing in the Himalayas.** **2 U**

An explanation which covers any two of these points would gain two marks:

Blatant lifts: 0.

1	he had only done a few climbs in Scotland (and some hillwalking)
2	he should have spent several winters practising in Scotland
3	he should have spent some winters climbing in the Alps
4	he should have done some big (new) (classic) climbs in the Alps

13 **Show how the imagery of lines 29–40 highlights the positive aspects of climbing on the particular day he is describing. You should consider at least two images.** **4 A**

Marks will depend on the quality of comment. Reference alone: 0. An insightful comment on one example could gain up to 3 marks; a more basic comment will be worth 1 mark. Two examples must be dealt with for full marks.

continued ➤

Mountains of the Mind

Answers on imagery must 'deconstruct' the image, i.e. show an understanding of the literal root of the image and then explore how the writer is extending it figuratively.

1	'appetite'	suggests that he was as eager to get to climbing as he was to eat when hungry
2	'crux'	the point of balance/the cross roads of a climb, the point at which success or failure happened
3	'lifted up like a surfer on a great wave of adrenalin'	as if the surge of adrenalin released into his body was acting as though he was being physically lifted up in the same way that a surfer is lifted by a wave
4	'needle-bright'	the air was sharp and brilliant like a shiny needle
5	'I felt like a king'	the impression of being at the top, master of the landscape, with great feelings of superiority
6	'the earth as Paradise'	what was below was new-minted, full of colour like the Garden of Eden in the beginning

14 **'The intensity we win through effort!' (line 41)**

(a) Explain what the writer means by this. **1 U**

There must be some attempt to use own words. Blatant lifts: 0.

the marvellous/memorable experiences/mood of euphoria we are rewarded with when we have gone to the extremes of physical endurance

(b) Show how word choice and sentence structure in lines 41–47 illustrate the intensity of the experience. **4 A**

Marks will depend on the quality of comment. Reference alone: 0. Mere identification of feature: 0. An insightful comment on one example/feature could score up to 3 marks; more basic comments could add up to 4. Both techniques must be dealt with for full marks.

Word choice:

1	'pristine (clarity)'	sense of newness uncorrupted
2	'mystical'	moves the experience into a spiritual dimension
3	'(orange segment) squirting'	(onomatopoetic) sensual word to enhance the experience
4	'(smell of it) filling the moment'	all pervading/invading sensual image
5	'(moments of) completeness'	spiritual sense creating wholeness of mind/body

continued ➤

Sentence structure:

6	exclamatory first sentence (line 41)	sense of excitement/discovery/euphoria
7	list of clauses in third sentence (lines 42–46)	many ordinary experiences transformed by becoming part of a single exceptional experience
8	use of semi-colons in lines 43–46	allows the reader to dwell on each moment/savour it
9	use of dash (line 46)	introduces the summing up of all these experiences/condenses them all into one
10	final short sentence (lines 46–47)	declarative/emphatic statement; not to be argued with; sums up the unforgettable nature of the experience

---

Question on both Passages

15 **Which passage do you feel creates more interest in the subject of mountaineering? By examining the ideas and the style of both passages justify your choice. In your discussion of style you might consider such features as tone, structure, imagery...**   **5 E**

Note that candidates must comment on ideas **and** style.

The mark for this question should reflect the overall quality of the response and may not be directly related to the length of the response or to the number of points/references made. A succinct, sophisticated response should be worth more than a series of fairly trivial points and obvious references. 'Ticking and adding up' is not appropriate (or fair) here.

For full marks there must be reference to both passages (although not necessarily a balanced treatment) and convincing evaluative comment. Where reference is made to one passage only, the maximum mark is 3.

The following guidelines should be used:

5 marks	clear and intelligent understanding of ideas and style in both passages; effective references; evaluative comment is convincing
4 marks	clear understanding of ideas and style in both passages; sensible references; evaluative comment is reasonably convincing
3 marks	understanding of ideas and style in both passages; adequate references; discernible evaluative comment

continued ➤

> Mountains of the Mind

2 marks   some understanding of ideas and/or style; limited reference; at least one
            appropriate evaluative comment

1 mark   one or two relevant but unconvincing comments.

Some of the following points might be touched on to provide material for this question:

Ideas:

Passage One:

introduction giving modern mountaineering a historical context

initial preference for tamed landscapes and perceptions of mountains as dangerous, barriers to
trade and travel – a practical view

development of scientific interest in mountains; the dawn of the romantic imagination;
increasing urbanisation and the desire to escape

leading to a more philosophical and spiritual appreciation (non-practical – mountains are still
dangerous)

the contradiction between the purely practical and physical entities which are mountains
(lumps of rock) and the concept of wilderness, danger, beauty reared in the imagination of
devotees of mountaineering

Passage Two:

personal narrative of the experience of climbing

analysis of Brit Style – obsession with climbing, initially fuelled by social aspects

inadequacy of his preparation, ambivalent feelings about the hard physical aspects of
climbing/fear etc.

but when all was well:

evocative description of one day's experience of mountains and the physical surroundings

incorporating the intense physical and spiritual experience; beauty, personal fulfilment

Style:

Passage One:

language of exposition with emphasis on the danger as well as the appeal

ideas explained, expounded, developed

vocabulary: formal scientific	'aesthetically repellent', 'culturally devised', 'contingencies', 'permeate', 'disjunction'…
tone – expository	'to the orthodox…'
– dramatic	'pulped rigid', 'fell to their deaths', 'the hand's touch'…
time linking – historical	'three centuries', '1700s', 'today'…

continued ➤

Mountains of the Mind

sentence structure (compact)	crafted, balanced, complex, use of single word triads
vivid/unusual imagery:	'brush of a bird's wing', 'blue jaws…'
effective opening and closing sentences	

Passage Two:

language of personal experience and emotion conjured up by evocative techniques

use of first person

vocabulary: more colloquial	'gleaming new gear', 'moaning and groaning', 'yomping'
tone – self-deprecating/humorous	'grand total', 'yomping', 'I had little problem…', 'Good Brit Style'
– intense	'dazzling world', 'mystical'…
time linking personal not historical	'as time went by', 'by the end of the season', 'one day'…
sentence structure (cumulative)	many short punchy sentences – 'But other days…'; lists to represent packed experience (e.g. line 17, line 43); longer triads for climax (line 7, line 18, line 37)
imagery (more immediate)	'surfer…' 'earth as Paradise', 'making the world fruit'…
effective opening and closing sentences